astrology
for beginners

ABOUT THE AUTHOR

Joann Hampar (New York) began her career in astrology in New York City when she was hired as a staff writer for *American Astrology* magazine. In the years that followed, she devoted much of her time to counseling private clients and writing freelance articles for magazines such as *Dell Horoscope*, *The Mountain Astrologer*, Llewellyn's *New Worlds of Mind & Spirit*, and AFA's *Today's Astrologer*. Her first book was published in 1993 by the American Federation of Astrologers and addressed a simplified method of reading a birth chart.

Hampar studied at the American School of Astrology in New York City and is certified in electional and horary astrology. She is currently a faculty member of the Online College of Astrology (www.astrocollege .com) and is a member of the American Federation of Astrologers, National Council for Geocosmic Research, Theosophical Society, Association for Research and Enlightenment, and Asia Society. Her other Llewellyn title is *Electional Astrology: The Art of Timing*.

Hampar resides in Manhattan and Montauk, New York, with her husband and cat. For more information, visit her at www.astroinsights.com.

Joann Hampar

astrology
for beginners

A SIMPLE WAY TO READ YOUR CHART

Llewellyn Publications
Woodbury, Minnesota

First Edition
First Printing, 2007

Book design and format by Donna Burch
Cover art © DigitalVision and Corel
Cover design by Ellen Dahl
Editing by Andrea Neff
Interior illustrations by Donna Burch
Llewellyn is a registered trademark of Llewellyn Worldwide, Ltd.

Chart wheels were produced by the Kepler program with the permission of Cosmic Patterns Software Inc. (www.AstroSoftware.com)

Library of Congress Cataloging-in-Publication Data
Hampar, Joann
     Astrology for beginners : a simple way to read your chart / by Joann
        Hampar.—1st ed.
     p. cm.
     ISBN-13: 978-0-7387-1106-5
     1. Astrology. I. Title.

    BF1708.1.H345 2007
    133.5—dc22   2007037806

Llewellyn Publications
A Division of Llewellyn Worldwide, Ltd.
2143 Wooddale Drive, Dept. 978-0-7387-1106-5
Woodbury, Minnesota 55125-2989, U.S.A.
www.llewellyn.com

Printed in the United States of America

OTHER BOOKS BY JOANN HAMPAR

Electional Astrology
(Llewellyn Publications, 2005)

How to Read Your Birth Chart
(American Federation of Astrologers, 1993)

ACKNOWLEDGMENTS

I would like to acknowledge Andrea Neff, whose queries and commentary enhanced the content of this book.

CONTENTS

CHARTS

chapter one

INTRODUCTION

Your birth chart, with its zodiac signs and planets, captures the precise moment in time when you were born. In fact, *horoscope* literally means "hour watcher," an observation of the hour of birth. This snapshot of the celestial bodies frozen in time is yours for life, and it will give you a lifetime of information. Exploring your horoscope need not be complicated, and in the following pages you will find all you need to simplify the process. Ideally, this language of symbols describes your life's fullest potential—and that's what this book is all about.

Each horoscope has a distinct blueprint, so we begin with a discussion of your chart pattern, providing an immediate overview of the driving force in your life. The signs of the zodiac and their placement in your birth chart show how you manage things. The twelve houses—each assigned a different topic—point to where you may achieve honors and success. The resources you have at your disposal, as defined by the planets, reveal family dynamics, personal and intimate relationships, finances and financial prospects, professional and vocational aptitudes, natural talents, creativity, and much more. If you have ever wondered what would be the best career choice or life path, the section on aspects will help identify your strongest career and vocational indicators.

When you first gaze at your horoscope, it's like discovering a secret map that will lead you on an exciting journey. And, like the circle that has no beginning and no end, your journey of self-discovery is an ever-unfolding adventure.

FRAMEWORK OF THE HOROSCOPE

The following outline describes the framework of the horoscope and illustrates how to use this book. It lists the interpretive techniques that are offered and explained in detail in the following chapters. These methods will give you easy access to the meaning of your horoscope. You do not need to understand complex theories or concepts. If you can identify the symbols, then you can understand your horoscope. In these pages, you will find everything you need, including lots of visual aids and charts to help you define your birth chart. At the end of the book is a comprehensive glossary.

It is best if you follow along with a copy of your horoscope. If you have never had your birth chart done, there are a number of Internet resources that provide free chart services. A few good ones are www .alabe.com, www.astro.com, and www.astrology.com. For those of you who do not have access to the Internet, you may complete the form at the back of this book to obtain a free copy of your birth chart. If you are not sure of your birth time, you may be able to obtain a time-stamped copy of your birth certificate by going to the National Center of Health Statistics website at http://www.cdc.gov/nchs/howto/w2w/w2welcom.htm.

I. The Seven Chart Patterns

The first thing you notice when you look at your horoscope is a pattern formed by the distribution of the planets. This chart pattern falls into one of seven categories, each with a specific meaning. It offers a broad view of the whole person, leading to a better understanding of the finer details. The pattern type, like a first impression, gives you an immediate picture of the driving force or motivational factors in your life.

A. The seven chart patterns: Splash, Bundle, Locomotive, Bowl, Bucket, Seesaw, and Splay.

B. Hemispheres: The next feature to note is whether the planets are mostly in the upper half or the lower half of the circle. Or you may notice that most of the planets are on the right-hand or left-hand side of the circle. This division of the circle into hemispheres describes inner and outer behavior.

C. Quadrants: The circle can be further divided into four quadrants that describe your developmental process and focus. Each of the four quadrants shows a particular area of life experience. The first quadrant is the realm of self-awareness; the second quadrant is related to creativity and talent; the third emphasizes relationships and interaction with others; and the fourth stresses profession/occupation, friendships, and humanitarian concerns.

II. The Twelve Signs of the Zodiac

Around the edges of the wheel are the twelve signs of the zodiac. Each of the twelve signs is unique in its expression and describes *how* you approach things. The signs also can be grouped according to certain similarities, such as element and quality.

A. Twelve zodiac signs: ♈ ♉ ♊ ♋ ♌ ♍ ♎ ♏ ♐ ♑ ♒ ♓

B. Four elements: fire, air, water, and earth—describe your basic nature

C. Three qualities: cardinal, fixed, and mutable—describe how you tend to act

D. Ascendant sign: describes your appearance and demeanor

III. The Twelve Houses

Each sign sits at the beginning of a house—on its *cusp*. Notice that the houses are numbered in the middle of the wheel in a counterclockwise direction. Each of the twelve houses describes a particular area of life experience, and the sign on its cusp illustrates how you approach that area of life.

A. Twelve houses

B. House position: angular, succedent, and cadent

C. Empty houses

D. Twelve signs through the twelve houses

IV. The Planets

The planets are dispersed around the wheel and reside in various houses. Each planet describes function or, to put it another way, something in particular about the way you carry out your life. The planet describes *what* is going on, while the house describes *where* the action occurs.

A. The ten planets: eight planets and two luminaries (the Sun and Moon)

B. The planets in the houses

C. The planets in the signs

V. The Aspects

Aspects are the angles between two planets or between a planet and any point on your horoscope. They are measured in degrees, and when planets form these angles, they interact with and reflect the influence of the other.

A. The five major aspects: conjunction, sextile, square, trine, and opposition

B. The ten planets and their primary aspects

C. Aspects to the Ascendant and Midheaven

So let's begin by examining the seven chart patterns to determine which one is closest to your own. Like a first impression, your birth chart pattern instantly reveals the essence of who you are. Then in the following chapters, we will look at the finer details of your horoscope.

chapter two

THE SEVEN CHART PATTERNS

The first thing you notice when you look at your horoscope wheel is that the planets are dispersed in such a way as to form a distinct pattern. This pattern has meaning in the broadest sense, defining the way you approach life. It offers a whole view of your being that is necessary before you begin the process of defining all its parts. In selecting which pattern is closest to your own, use only the ten planets. Your horoscope may not fit precisely into one specific pattern. In that case, look for the signature in each chart pattern that is the closest to your own.

As we discuss these chart patterns, keep in mind that the horoscope, like all circles, consists of 360 degrees, and each division of the circle is equal to 30 degrees, or one-twelfth of the whole. Later, we will define the twelve houses of the horoscope.

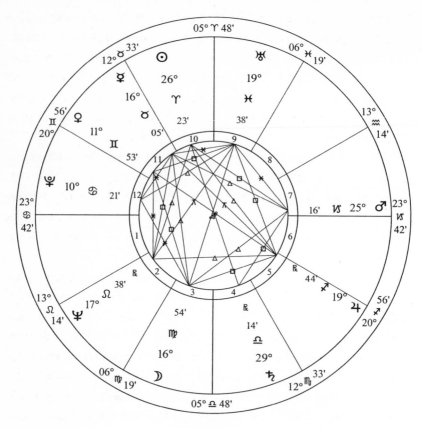

Henry Mancini
April 16, 1924 / 11:10 a.m. EST / Cleveland, Ohio
Placidus Houses

SPLASH PATTERN

Keywords: versatility, universality

Signature: planets in mostly different signs

The splash pattern has the planets dispersed around the wheel with most of the signs occupied. The component to look for is whether or not you have planets in mostly different signs. The splash pattern shows someone who has widespread interests, can do many different things, and is broad-minded and often spiritual or philosophical. There is an adventurous nature and an ability to perceive universal concepts. This horoscope pattern is seen regularly in the charts of those who contribute something to humanity, such as great scientists, prophets, composers, or even politicians. Theodore Roosevelt had a splash pattern and was known for his broad-based interest in many different subjects and people. He accomplished many noteworthy things during his presidency and was considered to have been a visionary.

The more negative expression of the splash pattern is a tendency to be somewhat scattered or to go in many directions at once. However, someone with this pattern has the capacity to grasp the big picture, often accompanied by an ability to implement sweeping concepts. The splash pattern shows a person who makes a noticeable difference in the lives of others and has humanitarian interests.

The birth chart of Henry Mancini is presented here as a rare example of a perfect splash pattern. Every planet occupies a different sign, and his life is a wonderful example of many of the characteristics associated with the splash pattern. Mancini was one of the all-time great composers and his contribution to music is distinguished. From the mid-1950s through the mid-1960s, he dominated both the film and television music scene when he wrote such hits as "Moon River" for *Breakfast at Tiffany's*, the theme song for *The Pink Panther*, and the theme song for *Peter Gunn*, a half-hour television crime drama. He was the most successful film composer of his time and earned both Academy and Grammy Awards. His versatility enabled him to compose music for many different genres, from dramas and musicals to motion pictures.

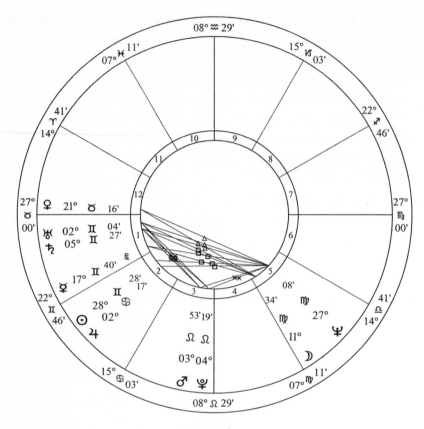

Brian Wilson
June 20, 1942 / 3:45 a.m. PWT / Inglewood, California
Placidus Houses

BUNDLE PATTERN

Keywords: concentration, focus

Signature: planets within 120 degrees, or one-third of the wheel

The bundle is what the name implies—all planets are huddled together, usually within the space of a trine, or 120 degrees. Quite often, this pattern exhibits a number of planets occupying the same sign, known as a *stellium*. This concentration of planets lends itself to a highly focused interest in one area and the ability to make the most of whatever circumstances may provide. The bundle shows someone who is self-contained and opportunistic and can master a particular area of interest. The person with this pattern often displays a strong sense of self-empowerment and a genius for impressing his or her ideas on others. Whether or not this power is used wisely is the difference between the visionary and the dictator. This pattern can produce great thinkers or, at its worst, someone bent on self-aggrandizement. Italian dictator Benito Mussolini had this pattern.

A contemporary example of the bundle pattern is seen in the birth chart of songwriter-musician Brian Wilson. His horoscope, presented here, is a good example of the bundle pattern at its best. Wilson was able to focus his considerable talent and energy on his goals. Throughout the 1960s, he was the driving force behind the Beach Boys. He was known to be a perfectionist in the studio, so much so that the other members of the group often had difficulty with his insistence on excellence. His highly focused drive and determination helped steer the group to great success around the world.

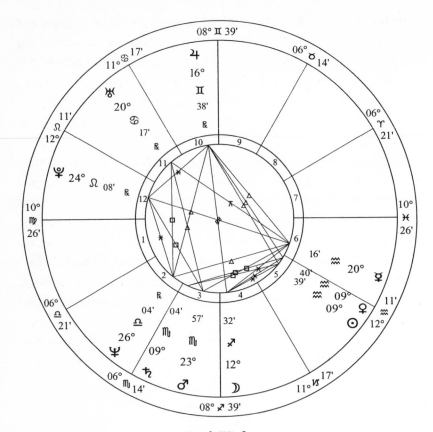

Oprah Winfrey
January 29, 1954 / 7:51 p.m. CST / Kosciusko, Mississippi
Placidus Houses

LOCOMOTIVE PATTERN

Keywords: confidence, individuality

Signature: planets in two-thirds of the wheel

The locomotive pattern shows planets dispersed around two-thirds of the wheel, leaving an empty trine, or space of 120 degrees. Someone with this pattern may be described as a self-driving individual whose persistence often results in great accomplishments. This often is complemented by a strong need to solve problems and to make a contribution to society as a whole. The personality can reflect an innate power to achieve one's goals, so this pattern usually is associated with executive ambition. Sometimes a strong desire to succeed can result in a rebellious nature. The person with this pattern usually is motivated by external factors associated with the *lead planet* in the pattern. To locate the lead planet, place your finger in the empty trine (empty space of 120 degrees) and move it counterclockwise. The first planet you see is the lead planet.

The chart presented here is that of Oprah Winfrey—businesswoman, talk show host, actress, and humanitarian. She is certainly an example of someone who feels she has a purpose in life and has chosen to focus her considerable energy on making a difference in the world. The driving power innate in this pattern is used to help others. The lead planet in her locomotive pattern is Jupiter, the planet of publishing, benevolence, generosity, and expansion. It is situated in her tenth house of career and in Gemini, the sign of communications. Her lead planet exemplifies the direction in which she has chosen to take her career. She is an inspiration to those who have had to overcome difficult circumstances and is an example of what can be accomplished when one believes in oneself.

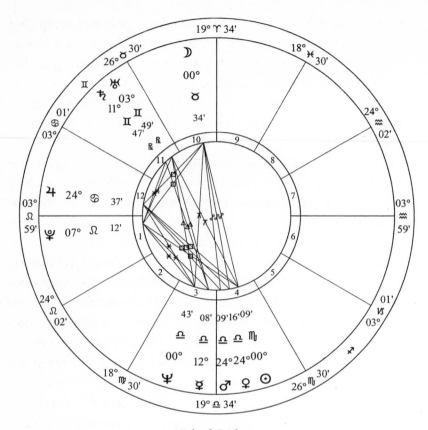

Michael Crichton
October 23, 1942 / 11:55 p.m. CWT / Chicago, Illinois
Placidus Houses

BOWL PATTERN

Keywords: independent, self-sufficient

Signature: planets in half the wheel

The bowl pattern shows planets occupying one half of the wheel. Someone with this pattern may be described as a person with strong inner resources and a desire to gather knowledge and further self-awareness. The person is independent and self-reliant and may feel set apart from others. This arises from the division between the occupied and unoccupied portions of the chart wheel. An awareness of something to bear in life or that certain experiences may be lacking often accompanies this chart pattern. For this reason, the individual shows a temperament directed toward furthering some cause or objective. The personality tends to be introspective, as the person seeks to know the purpose of life. A bowl holds something, and the native with this chart pattern always has something to give to others. The bowl pattern occurs frequently in the charts of those who make personal sacrifices to bring their vision to the world. Abraham Lincoln had a bowl pattern in his birth chart, with all the planets in the upper half of the wheel. This is the hemisphere associated with those who live an outer, objective life. History records the many personal sacrifices Lincoln made for his cause, that of protecting and defending the Union.

The chart illustrated here is that of Michael Crichton, best known as a writer of gripping science-related thrillers. Many of his books have become successful films, among them *Jurassic Park*. What is less well known is that he attended Harvard and graduated as a medical doctor. He is a very good example of the depth of character often seen in the bowl pattern individual. Here we see the desire to help others and share knowledge focused through his writing. He is also the creative force behind the hit NBC series *ER*. Crichton is certainly a seeker of knowledge. Much of the research that goes into his books draws upon his background and training in the medical and scientific fields. He is a prolific writer who seems to focus his considerable inner resources on the need to inform and entertain the masses.

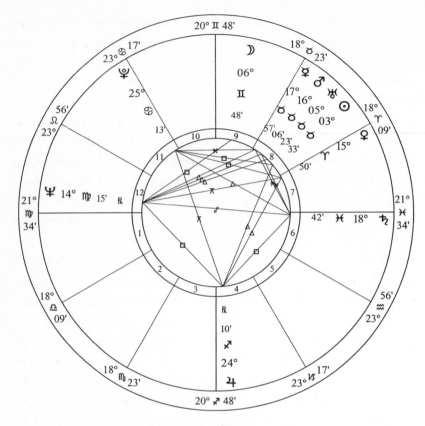

Roy Orbison
April 23, 1936 / 3:50 p.m. CST / Vernon, Texas
Placidus Houses

BUCKET PATTERN

Keywords: energetic, ambitious

Signature: an isolated planet

The bucket pattern is easy to spot, with one planet isolated from the rest, forming what looks like the handle of a bucket. The ideal bucket shows planets in half the wheel, with the singleton creating a T formation with two planets in opposition, as shown here. However, this is not always the case, so the element to look for is a planet isolated from the rest. In rare instances, the handle may be formed by two planets very close together, defined as a *conjunction*. But to be classified as a bucket, the conjunction must be exact or very close in orb (0–5°). (Orbs will be discussed in chapter 6.) The person with this pattern wants to experience life fully, and the area represented by the planet forming the handle usually represents a special capacity or intensified area of interest. Like the bowl, this pattern shows someone who accumulates experience but directs his or her considerable energy toward some pioneering venture. The handle planet reveals an important area of interest and often is associated with a special talent or gift in some creative area. The focus on that activity can be unwavering.

The horoscope illustrated here is that of singer-composer Roy Orbison. He was a pioneer of rock 'n' roll whose recording career spanned more than four decades, from the mid-1950s through the mid-1980s. Among his hits were "Only the Lonely," "Pretty Woman," and "Crying." The many planets in Taurus attest to his extraordinary vocal talents, but it is the focal planet, Jupiter, forming the handle of this bucket, that tells the real story. Orbison thought of himself as a writer first and a performer second. Here, the planet Jupiter in its own sign is evidence of his talent as a prolific writer of songs and his ability to explore new territory in that vein. He stretched the limits of his art by writing songs in a way that had not been done before. Likewise, his vocal talents were extraordinary, original, and unique, infusing the sound of country music with operatic flair. In this example, the singleton planet broadly defines Orbison's life. He was a creative artist who let his imagination soar and set the tone for those who followed in his footsteps. Throughout the years, he remained true to his style, never compromising or trying to adapt to what was trendy—Jupiter at its best.

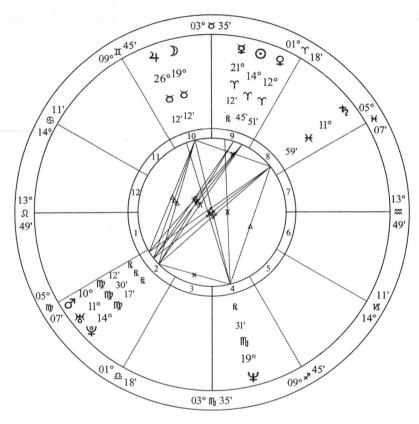

Robert Downey Jr.
April 4, 1965 / 1:10 p.m. EST / New York, New York
Placidus Houses

SEESAW PATTERN

Keywords: awareness, compromise

Signature: planets in opposing signs

The seesaw pattern shows two opposing groups of planets, with a space of at least 90 degrees on either side of the grouping. It reveals an individual striving to balance life experience from opposing points of view. The person with this pattern is capable of understanding both sides of an issue and will consider contrasting opinions before taking action. It often results in a life of conflict and compromise, where balance is the key to self-fulfillment. When balance is attained, there is the capacity for great accomplishment through an innate awareness of what others need.

The seesaw pattern shows someone who has many broad-based interests. Contrast and conflict present in the life of this individual result in a provocative personality, unafraid to challenge the status quo. At their best, those born with this chart pattern put an indelible mark on humanity, often leaving behind a significant contribution.

The birth chart presented here is that of actor Robert Downey Jr., best known for his role as Charlie Chaplin in the 1992 movie *Chaplin*. Both he and the character he portrayed in the film are good examples of a life of struggle and conflict giving rise to extraordinary accomplishment as expressed through each of their art forms. Downey received an Academy Award nomination for his brilliant portrayal of Chaplin. Interestingly, Charlie Chaplin's horoscope also contains many planets in opposition, though the pattern is not a true seesaw.

Robert Downey Jr. is an example of the disparate temperament often exhibited in someone with this pattern. Over a period of years, he has given consistently good and even brilliant performances in the movie roles he has taken, while at the same time his personal life has been plagued with self-destructive behavior. However, in recent years he has settled into a more balanced lifestyle and continues to work diligently at his craft. Downey appears to have found a peaceful coexistence with his own inner self, and most likely we will continue to be entertained by his exceptional talent for a long time to come.

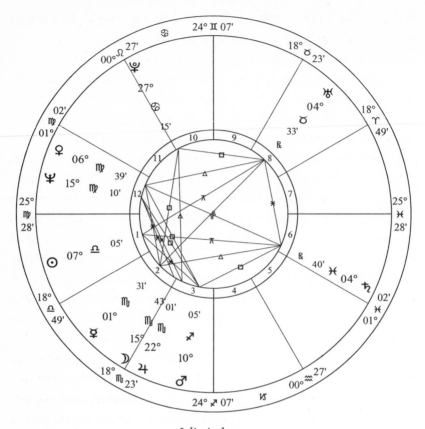

Julie Andrews
October 1, 1935 / 6:00 a.m. BST / Walton-on-Thames, England
Placidus Houses

SPLAY PATTERN

Keywords: artistic, self-reliant

Signature: irregular distribution of planets

The splay pattern is one in which the planets are distributed in an irregular fashion. If your chart pattern does not fit into any one of the other categories, it may be classified as a splay. It often will have three areas of emphasis, but not always, and shows a person who is not easily defined. Someone with this pattern has diverse interests and is capable of great accomplishments. This individual is often unconventional and resists being pigeonholed. A strong, often intense personality and a desire to achieve recognition are characteristics of this pattern.

The random distribution of the planets shows the varying points of interest in the character. This is someone who cannot be limited to one direction in life and is often accomplished in many areas. The person with a splay pattern is self-motivated and even cunning in his or her ability to take advantage of all opportunities that come along.

The horoscope illustrated here is that of the multitalented actress, singer, dancer, and performer Julie Andrews. She typifies the multidimensional personality and remarkable accomplishments of the splay pattern individual. Who can forget her wonderful performance as Mary Poppins for which she won her first Oscar, followed by *The Sound of Music*, one of the best-loved movies of all time. Though we know her best through her movies and stage performances, Andrews is also a successful author of children's books. She has received numerous awards throughout the years and in 2001 was honored at the John F. Kennedy Center for her unique and extremely valuable contribution to films and musical theater.

The characteristics of the splay chart are easily seen in the life of Julie Andrews. She has had a career that spans well over fifty years, and she continues to explore new projects. Her many talents and interests make it difficult to put her into any one category, so she personifies the temperament of her chart pattern.

THE FOUR HEMISPHERES

The circle that is the horoscope can be divided into hemispheres, each with a specific meaning. If you draw a horizontal line through the middle of the circle, the upper half is identified as the *southern hemisphere* and the lower half the *northern hemisphere*. Erase that line and now draw a vertical line through the center of the circle. The space on the right-hand side is identified as the *western hemisphere* and the space on the left-hand side is the *eastern hemisphere*. Note that the directions on the horoscope wheel are opposite the directions on a map.

The southern hemisphere is associated with qualities that are out in the open or easily visible. When the majority of planets appear in the upper half of the horoscope, the personality is generally extroverted, approachable, and receptive. These people tend to be in the public eye or to make choices that gain them recognition. Their lives are observable, and they are easily recognizable.

The northern hemisphere is associated with characteristics that are not easily visible. When the majority of planets are in the bottom half of the horoscope, the personality is somewhat concealed and the person tends to be private. These individuals are inner-directed and often go their own way. This doesn't mean that a public life is denied, but that they are less concerned with what others think. They are not easily defined and are less easily known.

The western hemisphere is associated with behavior that is responsive to others. When the majority of planets are located on the right-hand side of the horoscope, the person is likely to wait until an opportunity is offered. It is advantageous to respond to circumstances rather than initiate action. These people often will use their talents to benefit others. It is a pattern connected with those who interact and work best when in partnership or collaboration with others.

The eastern hemisphere is associated with behavior that is self-motivated. When the majority of planets are located on the left-hand side of the horoscope, the person is someone who initiates action. These are people who can work well alone, move ahead independently, and are likely to accomplish more on their own. This pattern shows individuals who succeed through their own efforts.

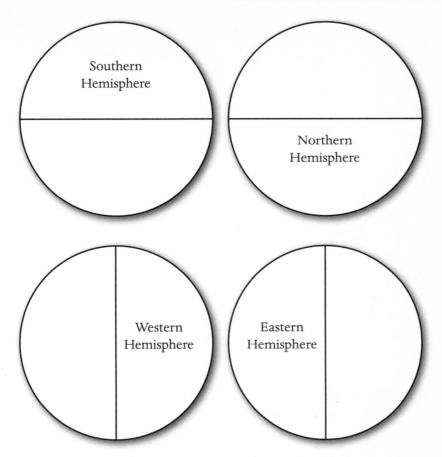

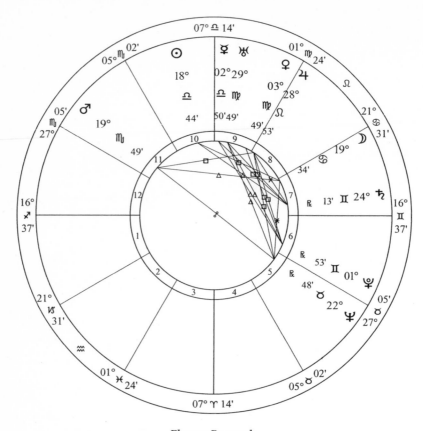

Eleanor Roosevelt
October 11, 1884 / 11:00 a.m. EST / New York, New York
Placidus Houses

Southern Hemisphere Emphasis

The chart of Eleanor Roosevelt, first lady of the United States during Franklin Roosevelt's extended presidency, shows a southern hemisphere emphasis in her horoscope. She was someone who was always in the public eye, and her personality was unguarded, honest, and open. Her constant work to improve the lives of people who are underprivileged made her one of the most beloved women of her generation. She greeted thousands with charming friendliness and enjoyed a long public career. Roosevelt lived her entire life in the public arena, and she was well respected for always expressing her opinions candidly.

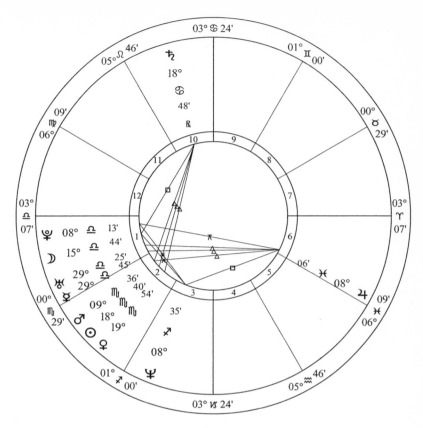

Leonardo DiCaprio
November 11, 1974 / 2:47 a.m. PST / Los Angeles, California
Placidus Houses

Northern Hemisphere Emphasis

We have a good example of a northern hemisphere emphasis in the horoscope of actor Leonardo DiCaprio. Though he is a well-known celebrity, his personality is more a projection of what he wishes the world to see, while his true character is not visible. As with the enigmatic Howard Hughes, whose life DiCaprio portrayed in the film *The Aviator*, we get the distinct impression that there is much about the actor that we do not know. There is an air of mystery in his demeanor, and he takes great pains to keep his personal life under wraps. He is someone who follows his own guidance, and, unlike most celebrities, avoids the public spotlight.

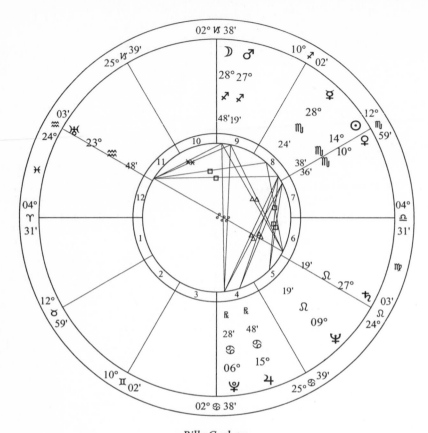

Billy Graham
November 7, 1918 / 3:30 p.m. EST / Charlotte, North Carolina
Placidus Houses

Western Hemisphere Emphasis

We have an ideal example of someone who is responsive to the needs of others in the chart of charismatic preacher Billy Graham. The predominance of planets in the western hemisphere describes a receptive, reactive individual who is accessible to people. The best-known Christian evangelist of the twentieth century, Graham founded ministries that continue to aid those in need worldwide. Often referred to as "the nation's preacher," he has consulted with every U.S. president from Dwight Eisenhower to George W. Bush.

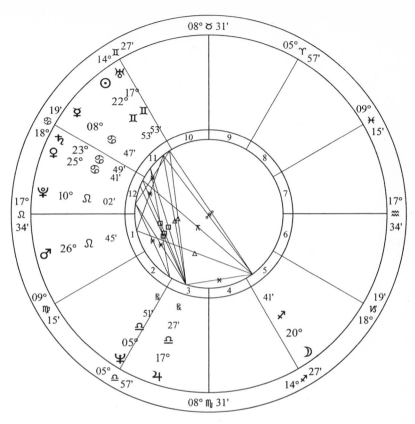

Donald Trump
June 14, 1946 / 9:51 a.m. EDT / Queens, New York
Placidus Houses

Eastern Hemisphere Emphasis

We see a perfect example of the self-motivated personality at its best in the birth chart of entrepreneur and real estate developer Donald Trump. His flair for self-publicity has made him a celebrity of sorts. The majority of his planets in the eastern hemisphere shows his ability to initiate action and move ahead independently. He rarely concerns himself with what others think and has the ability to stay focused on his personal goals, a characteristic of this pattern.

THE FOUR QUADRANTS

A further division of the circle into four equal parts brings us to the quadrants of the horoscope. You will notice that they are numbered in a counterclockwise direction. Each quadrant is associated with a particular area of focus, and when we find a majority of planets in any one quadrant, we can add the following meanings.

The first quadrant is the area of personal interests. When many planets are in this part of the horoscope, it describes a self-seeking individual whose resources are used for personal gain. The person's interests and use of talents and skills are focused on the self and on direct experience. This is not to imply a selfish approach to life; however, the developmental process is inner-directed. In the previous chart examples, Leonardo DiCaprio fits into this category.

The second quadrant is the area of the horoscope focused on creativity. Someone with many planets in this part of the horoscope is productive and often artistic. The focus is on creating something, whether it is a home and family, a manuscript, or some other imaginative project. Work also is important, and the person with a strong second quadrant may be focused on occupational interests. There can be a strong attraction to work of a service nature, such as social work or health care.

The third quadrant is the area of the chart referred to as the relationship area. Those with a majority of planets in this part of the horoscope prefer to interact with others; therefore, personal and business relationships are an important part of life. Someone with a strong third quadrant often will work with people to help them improve their financial or spiritual resources. There can be an interest in distant lands and foreign cultures or spiritual and philosophical matters. In the previous chart examples, Billy Graham fits into this category.

The fourth quadrant of the horoscope is termed the universal quadrant. Someone with many planets in this part of the chart is often ambitious and interested in career and reputation as well as the social order. This person can be a leader in the community, a corporate executive,

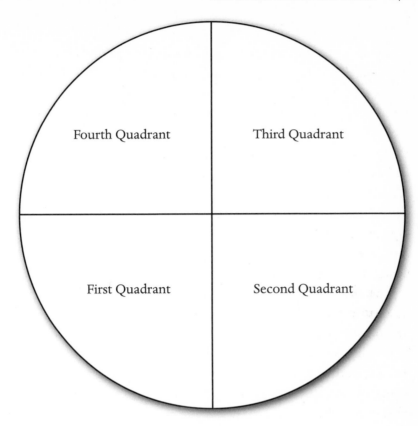

and/or active in collective group interests. Often, humanitarian activities are balanced with the need to establish a place in society. Recognition is usually sought after. In the previous chart examples, Donald Trump falls into this category.

chapter three

THE TWELVE SIGNS OF THE ZODIAC

Around the edges of the chart wheel are the twelve signs of the zodiac (see illustration on next page). Each one is unique in its expression and defines *how* you approach things. The sign sits on the cusp of a house and describes your attitude toward that area of life experience. The cusps are the lines separating each house and resemble the spokes of a wheel. Before we go further, let us define the symbolic language of astrology: (1) the signs describe *how* you do something, (2) the planets describe *what* you do or what is being expressed, and (3) the houses describe *where* things happen. When you combine the meanings of all three, you have a fundamental sense of astrology and a definition of the horoscope.

Almost everyone is familiar with their Sun sign. This is the sign the Sun occupied on the day you were born, and it is descriptive of certain characteristics of your personality. In this symbolic language, the Sun describes an important part of your being, but it is not the whole picture. Each of the other planets has meaning, and, like the Sun, each embodies the characteristics of the sign it occupied on the day you were born. Taken together, these symbols reflect the portrait of your life. But

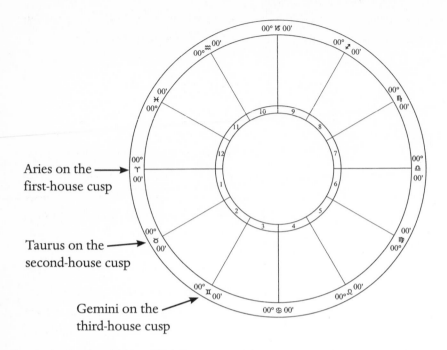

Aries on the → first-house cusp

Taurus on the → second-house cusp

Gemini on the → third-house cusp

before we get too far ahead of ourselves, let's examine the signs of the zodiac and take a look at the qualities associated with each one.

The zodiac signs can be grouped according to certain similarities. One is by element. The four elements are fire, earth, air, and water. The element describes the basic temperament of the sign. There is an obvious correlation between the element and its nature. Fire signs are enthusiastic, inspirational, and immediate. Earth signs are practical, stable, and deliberate. Air signs are inquisitive, questioning, and informative. Water signs are emotional, intuitive, and sustaining.

The signs also can be grouped by quality. The quality describes the basic energy or force behind it and the way it operates. The three qualities are cardinal, fixed, and mutable. Cardinal signs are active and take the lead. Fixed signs are steady and stay on course. Mutable signs are flexible and adapt to circumstances.

Every element and quality will appear somewhere in your horoscope. Regardless of your Sun sign or what planets occupy which signs in your horoscope, you share with every other human being on the planet the same underlying attributes that compose the universe.

THE FOUR ELEMENTS

Fire Signs: ♈ *Aries,* ♌ *Leo,* ♐ *Sagittarius*

The fire signs are energetic and enthusiastic and have a joy for life. The fire signs can inspire others with their optimism. They are direct, energetic, and outgoing and seldom let obstacles get in the way of what they want. Fire is intuitive and quick to act, and fire signs often charge forward without restraint. Wherever you have a fire sign in your horoscope, you may be impulsive and likely to take chances.

Earth Signs: ♉ *Taurus,* ♍ *Virgo,* ♑ *Capricorn*

The earth signs are practical, physical, and concerned with the material aspects of life. The earth signs rely on what can be verified and are not easily persuaded. They provide the foundation needed to establish something. They are patient, responsible, and persistent. Wherever you have an earth sign in your horoscope, you will work hard, plan carefully, and be less likely to take chances.

Air Signs: ♊ *Gemini,* ♎ *Libra,* ♒ *Aquarius*

The air signs represent the mental plane, and they are gatherers of knowledge. They never can have enough information and always want to know more. They seem detached because they are analytical rather than emotional. Wherever you have an air sign in your horoscope, you accumulate information, enjoy sharing ideas, and are always interested in knowing more.

Water Signs: ♋ *Cancer,* ♏ *Scorpio,* ♓ *Pisces*

The water signs are emotional, responsive, and instinctive. The water signs seem to know things intuitively. They want to take care of everyone and envelop those they care about. They feel things deeply and are often overprotective and oversensitive. The water signs struggle with emotions and can be moody. Wherever you have a water sign in your horoscope, you will follow your instincts.

THE THREE QUALITIES

The qualities—cardinal, fixed, and mutable—describe behavior. Cardinal signs want to lead and like to take the initiative. The keyword for the cardinal signs is action.

The fixed signs prefer to establish something permanent, so they are slow to act, but once they do, there's no stopping them. The keyword for the fixed signs is persistence.

Mutable signs are adaptable and want to discuss everything thoroughly before making a decision; the more information, the better. The keyword for the mutable signs is flexibility.

Cardinal Signs: ♈ Aries, ♋ Cancer, ♎ Libra, ♑ Capricorn

Aries, the fire element of the cardinal signs, is the sign of action and new beginnings. It is forceful, direct, and quick to act. Fire burns rapidly, so impatience is a strong characteristic of this sign. Aries individuals can appear to be brash, but it is their enthusiasm and thirst for adventure that enables them to go where others fear to tread. They have a strong need to break new ground and are often ahead of the trend.

The key phrase for Aries is "I am." This is the self-directed urge to experience things firsthand. Aries individuals are fearless and charge right in, overcoming whatever obstacles are in their way. Wherever you have Aries in your horoscope, you are assertive and direct and can take immediate action. This is where you won't back down.

Cancer is the water element of the cardinal signs. It is the sign of instinct, and Cancer individuals can be tenacious about what they want. This is the sign of the mother—the nurturing quality that emotionally sustains us. Cancer individuals love to take care of everything and everyone who needs help. Water is the element that envelops all it touches, and Cancer individuals can be overly protective. It is hard for them to let go.

The key phrase for Cancer is "I feel." Like the ocean tides that ebb and flow, Cancer individuals are restless and want to roam. They also are very psychic and absorb the feelings of those around them. Wherever you find

Cancer in your horoscope, you are intuitive, sensitive, and restless. You may change your mind and go with your instincts.

Libra is the air element of the cardinal signs. It is the sign of interaction with others and therefore rules relationships. Librans are always interested in both sides of an issue and are balanced and unbiased. Good manners and social graces are important to Librans, and they rarely act by themselves. They prefer doing things jointly. The development of relationships is the most important function for Libra.

The key phrase for Libra is "I balance." Air is the element of intellect, so wherever you find Libra in your horoscope, you seek balance through understanding. Partnership is important, so you will gravitate toward making decisions jointly with others. This is where you seek fairness and harmony.

Capricorn is the earth element of the cardinal signs. It is the sign of organization, structure, and planning. Capricorns are persistent and patient and know how to make the most of something. They are capable of great strength and perseverance. Capricorns are careful and calculated in their actions and generally accomplish their goals through sheer determination.

The key phrase for Capricorn is "I use." This is the sign that knows how to utilize whatever or whoever is at hand to accomplish the goal. Earth is solid and tangible, so wherever you find Capricorn in your horoscope, you can establish something permanent. You are likely to be quite organized, efficient, and careful in this area of your life.

Fixed Signs: ♉ Taurus, ♌ Leo, ♏ Scorpio, ♒ Aquarius

Taurus is the earth element of the fixed signs. Those born under this sign enjoy all of life's pleasures. They are tolerant to a fault and will put up with a lot. Taurus is the most fixed of the fixed signs. It is the sign of inertia, so Taurus individuals are slow to get started, but once they do, there's no stopping them. They have such strong determination that when they commit to something, they will not change course. You cannot persuade them otherwise and will meet with strong resistance if you try to change their minds.

The key phrase for Taurus is "I have." Taurus individuals are very attached to physical things and pleasures. Wherever you find Taurus in your horoscope, you are determined and tenacious. This is where you are most attached to things and won't give in.

Leo is the fire element of the fixed signs. Those born under this sign are warmhearted and enjoy being the center of attention. As with all the fixed signs, Leos like to possess things, and only the finest quality will do. Leos insist upon excellence, and like the Sun, which is the center of our solar system, they like to be in the center of things and have others revolve around them. They are courageous, confident, and loyal.

The key phrase for Leo is "I will." This is the sign of show business, and Leos are showy, playful, and entertaining. Wherever you have Leo in your horoscope, you crave attention. This is where you want to express yourself, put your best foot forward, and be recognized for your efforts.

Scorpio is the water element of the fixed signs. Those born under this sign are excellent at ferreting out the truth in any situation. They are unrelenting when it comes to discovering something they want to know but are quite secretive about their own lives. Scorpios struggle to transform some aspect of themselves. This is the sign of secrets, power, and intensity.

The key phrase for Scorpio is "I create." Scorpio is the sign of healing, death, and rebirth. It is called the mystery sign because there is much that is hidden. Wherever you have Scorpio in your horoscope, you have the desire to create. This is where you are likely to take control. You are able to get to the core of the matter.

Aquarius is the air element of the fixed signs. It is the sign of friendship, and those born under this sign value friends above all else. They often are unusual in the way they conduct themselves and like to be recognized for their efforts. Aquarians are always trying to stretch the boundaries, and they often are labeled rebellious in the process. "Out with the old and in with the new" is their philosophy.

The key phrase for Aquarius is "I know." This is the sign associated with everything strange and unusual, but it also is the sign of genius.

Wherever it is in your horoscope, you have the potential to transcend the ordinary. Aquarius is also the sign of social conscience, and this is where you are interested in making a difference.

Mutable Signs: ♊ Gemini, ♍ Virgo, ♐ Sagittarius, ♓ Pisces

Gemini is the air element of the mutable signs. It is the sign of communication, and Geminis love to do just that. There is no end to the amount of information they have at their fingertips or to the questions they ask. They are curious and intelligent and enjoy varied interests. "Here today, gone tomorrow" describes Gemini. They dislike routine, value their freedom, and have a hard time with commitment.

The key phrase for Gemini is "I think." Wherever you have Gemini in your horoscope, you seek awareness through many varied experiences. This is where the flow of information is important and where your thirst for knowledge never ceases.

Virgo is the earth element of the mutable signs. Those born under this sign collect and correlate facts. They are able to assimilate incredible amounts of detailed information. Their greatest fault is in being too critical. Virgo is the sign of analysis, work, and service. Virgos have the unique ability to see minute details and never miss a thing. They also desire to be of service and to reach the highest levels of perfection within themselves.

The key phrase for Virgo is "I analyze." Wherever Virgo is in your horoscope, you like to keep busy. This is where you can provide a service for or be of help to others. It is also where you are most critical.

Sagittarius is the fire element of the mutable signs. Those born under this sign are outspoken and just say what they think without hesitation. They are friendly, outgoing, and optimistic. Sagittarians like to take risks and are drawn to distant horizons. They often seek adventure through travel and like to tell stories about their explorations. They are independent, and freedom is very important to them.

The key phrase for Sagittarius is "I perceive," because they are seekers of knowledge and wisdom. Wherever you have Sagittarius in your horoscope, you are more likely to be adventurous, take risks, and seek broader understanding.

Pisces is the water element of the mutable signs. Those born under this sign believe their dreams will come true. This is the sign of faith, and Pisces is the most sensitive of all the signs. Imagination and creativity are strong in Pisces individuals. They hate to offend others and are so agreeable that they can appear to be insincere. They have a hard time saying what they really mean. Pisces individuals can suffer from a sense of unworthiness and never feel that they have done enough.

The key phrase for Pisces is "I believe." Wherever you have Pisces in the horoscope, you are tolerant and compassionate. This is also where you may be imaginative, dreamy, or unrealistic. You may sacrifice a lot in this area of your life.

NATURAL SEQUENCE OF THE TWELVE SIGNS

The signs always will appear in the same order in your horoscope wheel. The twelve signs we use in astrology correspond with a narrow belt of space in the sky referred to as the *zodiac*. Aries always is followed by Taurus, followed by Gemini, followed by Cancer, followed by Leo, and so on. The natural order of the signs is shown in the following chart.

Sequence	Glyph	Sign	Key Phrase	Ruling Planet	Symbol
1	♈	Aries	I am	Mars	Ram
2	♉	Taurus	I have	Venus	Bull
3	♊	Gemini	I think	Mercury	Twins
4	♋	Cancer	I feel	Moon	Crab
5	♌	Leo	I will	Sun	Lion
6	♍	Virgo	I analyze	Mercury	Virgin
7	♎	Libra	I balance	Venus	Scales
8	♏	Scorpio	I create	Pluto	Scorpion
9	♐	Sagittarius	I perceive	Jupiter	Centaur
10	♑	Capricorn	I use	Saturn	Goat
11	♒	Aquarius	I know	Uranus	Water Bearer
12	♓	Pisces	I believe	Neptune	Fish

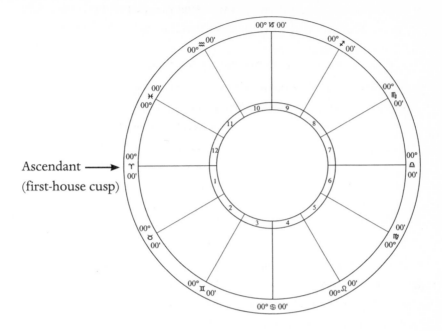

Ascendant ⟶
(first-house cusp)

The signs always are read counterclockwise on the wheel. You begin at the Ascendant, or first-house cusp, and proceed counterclockwise around the wheel. The cusps are the lines that divide the wheel into twelve houses. The sign that resides on the first-house cusp is your Ascendant sign. The second-house cusp will display the next sign in the natural sequence of the zodiac. Your Ascendant sign is as important as your Sun sign and describes your appearance and persona. It is what others see when they first meet you.

The Ascendant is determined by the time of birth. In the absence of a correct birth time, you can place your Sun sign on the Ascendant, followed by the signs in the natural sequence of the zodiac. This is referred to as a *solar chart*, or *Sun sign chart*, and will provide a wealth of information.

The sign on your Ascendant describes your persona, physical characteristics, and appearance. It is your outer shell and the first impression others have of you. It is the window through which you view the world. But more than that, it describes the qualities you cultivate and assimilate into your personality. These qualities are continually evolving and becoming part of your nature.

The chart on page 36 also lists the ruling planet of each sign. The ruling planet is the planet associated with a particular sign. When a planet is in the first house and particularly when it is close to the Ascendant, its influence is strong and your personality will reflect both the meaning of the Ascendant sign and the meaning of the planet.

YOUR ASCENDANT SIGN

♈ Aries on the Ascendant

The Aries Ascendant gives an outgoing personality—one who is energetic and impulsive. If you have this cardinal fire sign on the Ascendant, you express enthusiasm, impatience, and a zest for life. You are not easily deterred, and when presented with a challenge, you rise to the occasion. Always seeking the next adventure, you are quick to lose interest once the excitement wears off. If you have Aries on the Ascendant or Mars (the ruling planet of Aries) in the first house, you should surround yourself with others who can pick up where you left off. Aries is the sign of new beginnings and is best at getting things started; then it is up to others to complete the task.

♉ Taurus on the Ascendant

The Taurus Ascendant shows a quiet personality—one who is strong, steady, and cannot be pushed. If you have this fixed earth sign on the Ascendant, your appearance is serene, and you demonstrate patience and stamina. You are one who holds fast to your commitments, and you work hard to build a comfortable life for yourself and your loved ones. Your steadiness is comforting to others, and you often may find yourself in the role of counselor. With Taurus on the Ascendant or Venus (the ruling planet of Taurus) in the first house, you may be creative, talented, and artistic. Taurus is the sign of values, and when it is on the Ascendant, it helps you define what is of value. Money and possessions will be important.

♊ *Gemini on the Ascendant*

The Gemini Ascendant shows a friendly, talkative, and charming personality. If you have this mutable air sign on the Ascendant, information is of the utmost importance and you never can have enough. At times you may feel pulled in two directions as you struggle to integrate certain aspects of your personality. You have a witty charm and a way with words, making you the life of the party. Always on the go, you prefer to keep busy and may find it difficult to relax. At times you can take on too much, leaving you overwhelmed. With Gemini on the Ascendant or Mercury (the ruling planet of Gemini) in the first house, you are likely to have good communication skills and a knack for writing.

♋ *Cancer on the Ascendant*

The Cancer Ascendant gives a shy and sensitive outer shell. If you have this cardinal water sign on the Ascendant, you will make decisions based on feelings. Strong intuition can be characterized as a sixth sense, giving you the ability to tap into what others are feeling. With Cancer on the Ascendant or the Moon (the ruler of Cancer) in the first house, you are responsive and receptive to the needs of others. Your face may appear round, reflective of the full Moon. You may be restless, moody, or easily hurt, partly because you tend to take things too personally. A Cancer Ascendant is helpful in sensing public opinion; you may be involved with community, civic, or social issues.

♌ *Leo on the Ascendant*

The Leo Ascendant gives a friendly and self-confident personality, one who walks with pride and assurance. If you have this fixed fire sign on the Ascendant, you are courageous and don't mind taking risks. Strong vitality and a positive outlook keep you going well into your later years. When Leo is on the Ascendant or the Sun (the ruler of Leo) is in the first house, you may roar from time to time but will never hold a grudge. Conscious of your image and reputation, you take great pride in everything you do. Should others fail to appreciate your efforts, you may feel wounded. You do not take kindly to criticism and will never forget a snub.

♍ *Virgo on the Ascendant*

The Virgo Ascendant gives an alert mind and youthful appearance; you always look younger than your years. If you have this mutable earth sign on the Ascendant, you are practical and willing to work at something until it's perfect. You have a quiet and refined demeanor and a desire to be of help to others. With Virgo on the Ascendant or Mercury (the ruling planet of Virgo) in the first house, you are analytical and methodical in everything you do. You can be ingenious or self-critical and may feel your efforts are never quite good enough. An inquisitive nature and an interest in so many things keep you young at heart.

♎ *Libra on the Ascendant*

The Libra Ascendant gives a charming personality and an artistic and creative flair. If you have this cardinal air sign on the Ascendant, your nature is to seek balance through understanding. You strive to see both sides of an issue, yet you can debate your point with finesse. Librans often are found in the legal profession. With Libra on the Ascendant or Venus (the ruling planet of Libra) in the first house, you cannot thrive in an inharmonious environment. You prefer to avoid disagreements and may try too hard to please others, to your own detriment. You can be indecisive for fear of making a mistake. Your interest in people and natural social skills attract many friends.

♏ *Scorpio on the Ascendant*

The Scorpio Ascendant gives a disarmingly magnetic personality and an emotional intensity that is somewhat hidden. If you have this fixed water sign on the Ascendant, your emotions are deep and often are misunderstood. Powerful is the keyword for those with Scorpio on the Ascendant. You are soft-spoken, courageous, independent, and self-reliant. You can struggle to transform some aspect of yourself—there is a devil-angel mentality. With Scorpio on the Ascendant or Pluto (the ruling planet of Scorpio) in the first house, you are apt to hide your true feelings. Even when you implicitly trust someone, you are cautious. Strength, determination, and focus enable you to achieve your goals.

♐ Sagittarius on the Ascendant

The Sagittarius Ascendant gives an outgoing personality and a candor that often catches people off-guard. If you have this mutable fire sign on the Ascendant, you are always looking toward new horizons. You may prefer casual contacts to in-depth relationships and have many acquaintances but fewer friends. With Sagittarius on the Ascendant or Jupiter (the ruling planet of Sagittarius) in the first house, your optimism inspires others, and you may be found helping those who cannot help themselves. Fair-minded, you believe in equality for all. Freedom is important, and you avoid settling down. You love to take chances and live life to the fullest.

♑ Capricorn on the Ascendant

The Capricorn Ascendant gives a serious, mature personality; often there were difficult circumstances early in life. If you have this cardinal earth sign on the Ascendant, you are a natural leader who can overcome obstacles others would find daunting. You have great ambition and achieve your goals through sheer determination. With Capricorn on the Ascendant or Saturn (the ruling planet of Capricorn) in the first house, you are more sensitive than you let on and, like your symbol, the goat, will keep climbing until you reach your goals. You are ethical and responsible, with a strong sense of duty. Money and position are important, and once you make a commitment to something, it is as good as done.

♒ Aquarius on the Ascendant

The Aquarius Ascendant gives a positive, stimulating, and somewhat unusual personality. If you have this fixed air sign on the Ascendant, your enthusiasm inspires others. You are intuitive and original and have an eclectic interest in many different subjects, some of which may be unusual—like astrology, for instance. With Aquarius on the Ascendant or Uranus (the ruling planet of Aquarius) in the first house, you prefer to be left to your own creative devices. You cannot bear conformity and will go your own way. Anything that is new or cutting-edge appeals to you, and your insights may be at the forefront of change. You can be rebellious if challenged.

♓ *Pisces on the Ascendant*

The Pisces Ascendant gives a gentle, thoughtful personality. If you have this mutable water sign on the Ascendant, you are receptive to those around you and sensitive to your environment. Empathetic and intuitive, you can be overwhelmed by too much input. Spending time alone helps you maintain inner balance. With Pisces on the Ascendant or Neptune (the ruling planet of Pisces) in the first house, you have strong psychic perception and a desire to help people. You may have musical talent or other artistic inclinations. You are romantic and have a tendency to dream your dreams rather than live them. However, when you believe in yourself, your dreams can come true.

chapter four

THE TWELVE HOUSES

The horoscope is divided into twelve houses, and each one takes up a space of 30 degrees, or one-twelfth of the 360-degree circle. The lines that separate the houses are called *cusps*. Each house describes a different area of your life. The planets reside in the houses, and while the planets define *what* you do or what is being expressed, the houses describe *where* things take place. The houses are numbered 1 through 12, beginning at the center left-hand side of the wheel and proceeding counterclockwise. Each house has similarities to its corresponding sign. For instance, sign number seven, Libra, is the sign of marriage and partnership; thus, in your horoscope, house number 7 shows your marriage partner, relationships, and partnerships. Sign number four, Cancer, is the sign of home and family; therefore, house number 4 corresponds with that area of your life.

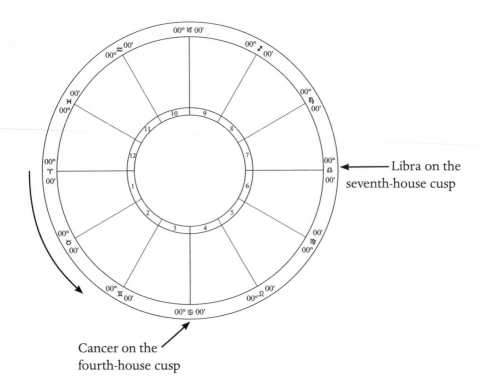

Libra on the
seventh-house cusp

Cancer on the
fourth-house cusp

FIRST HOUSE

The sign on the first-house cusp is your Ascendant sign and describes what you look like and how you express yourself. It shows your personality, disposition, and point of view. It defines the outer you, whereas your Sun sign describes the inner you. The first house is related to your physical characteristics, your appearance, the way you dress, wear your hair, and so on. Your health also is shown here. The first house indicates the way you approach new initiatives. Any planet in the first house will be a dominant influence in your life.

SECOND HOUSE

The second house is the house of money, possessions, and personal resources. It shows the value you place on yourself and what you have to offer others. This is also the house of your personal desires, and the sign on its cusp describes how you pursue your desires. The second house illustrates personal income; financial gain; valuables and assets. The sign on its cusp describes your attitude toward money. Any planet in the second house affects the way you handle your resources and money.

THIRD HOUSE

The third house describes the way you think and communicate, including writing and speaking. It is the house of the mind. As with many of the houses, the third house has multiple meanings. It describes your siblings, neighborhood, surroundings, and neighbors. It is also the house of elementary education and short journeys. The sign on its cusp defines how you communicate, express your ideas, and gather information. Any planet in this house influences the way you think, form conclusions, and convey your thoughts.

FOURTH HOUSE

The fourth house describes your home, family, and the environment during the formative years of your life. It describes your residence, property, and real estate. What's more, it defines your inner nature or soul and has come to be known as the root of your being. The fourth house shows the parent of lesser influence, whereas the more prominent parent is shown by the tenth house. The sign on the fourth-house cusp shows how you relate to a parent and to domestic affairs. Any planet in this house will influence your family relationships.

FIFTH HOUSE

The fifth house is the house of children and creativity. It includes anything you put forth that is creative, such as writing, sculpting, painting, and designing. This house further defines love, romance, and your emotional and romantic tendencies. What's more, it is the house of speculation, games of chance, hobbies, and sports. The sign on this cusp describes how you relate to children. Any planet in the fifth house will influence your romantic relationships and your children.

SIXTH HOUSE

The sixth house is the house of work and service. It defines the manner and setting in which you work, not your career. It shows routine matters or work that you have to perform on a regular basis. Moreover, it describes health-related issues. The sixth house also defines the nature of service given and received, so it includes those you employ to perform a service. The sign on its cusp describes how you approach your work and relate with co-workers. Any planet in this house further defines the nature of your work.

SEVENTH HOUSE

The seventh house is the house of relationships, marriage, and partnerships. It also defines business partners and cooperative interaction with others. Moreover, this is the house of open enemies, and though that may seem at odds with the house of marriage, it's not; when a relationship sours, hostility often ensues. The sign on the seventh-house cusp shows how you relate to a partner. Any planet in this house further defines relationships.

EIGHTH HOUSE

The eighth house is the house of regeneration (sex) and degeneration (death). Moreover, this is the house of renewal, which involves a broadening point of view or understanding. The eighth house describes other people's money, values, and possessions, including those of your spouse or partner. It can indicate money from an inheritance. Another domain is psychic sensitivity; those with planets here often can see, hear, or sense dead people. The sign on the eighth-house cusp describes how you utilize the resources of others.

NINTH HOUSE

The ninth house is the house of mental perception, higher education, philosophy, law, and religion. It shows your principles, aspirations, and growth—both mentally and spiritually. Moreover, it defines that which inspires and sustains you. It describes long journeys, air travel, and distant horizons. Your dealings with attorneys and legal affairs are shown in the ninth house. The sign on its cusp shows how you express your highest ideals. Any planet in this house will help to define your principles and beliefs.

TENTH HOUSE

The tenth house is the house of career, vocation, honors, and public image. It defines your reputation and standing in society. It shows what you want to achieve and your long-term objectives. The tenth house is the primary consideration in determining a career path. Moreover, it describes the parent of greater influence and is opposite the fourth house, which defines the parent of lesser influence. The sign on the tenth-house cusp describes how you are perceived by your peers. Any planet in this house can influence your career path.

ELEVENTH HOUSE

The eleventh house is the house of friendships, hopes, and wishes. It shows the kinds of friends you have and the things you hope and wish for. It describes relationships with groups of people, social connections, memberships, fraternities, and clubs and other organizations you choose to be part of. Moreover, it shows money earned from career or vocation. The sign on its cusp defines how you relate to your friends. Any planet in the eleventh house has a bearing on career income.

TWELFTH HOUSE

The twelfth house is the house of solitude, secrets, and hidden things. It often is referred to as the house of drawn shades. It describes those experiences that test us, such as confinement in a hospital or institution. Moreover, the twelfth describes limiting circumstances, such as caring for a parent or someone in need. In that vein, it is referred to as the house of restrictions. When this house is occupied, the individual is inclined to live a more solitary life or engage in activities that require solitude, like writing or spiritual practices. The sign on its cusp describes how you spend your solitary time.

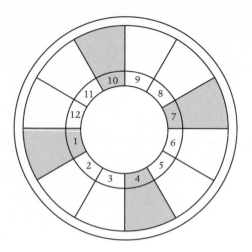

ANGULAR HOUSES

The angular houses are houses 1, 4, 7, and 10. They correspond with the cardinal signs of the same number: (1) Aries, (4) Cancer, (7) Libra, and (10) Capricorn. These are the houses where you can take action and see immediate results. If you have a majority of planets in the angular houses, you display many of the cardinal qualities. You prefer to take the initiative and tend to be an action-oriented individual; the focus is on getting things done without delay. You are impatient, ambitious, and restless. This pattern often is seen in the charts of corporate executives or high achievers.

We have a good example of angular-house emphasis in the horoscope of Bill Gates. He has five planets in angular houses 1, 4, and 10 and certainly can be defined as an active, let's-get-it-done-now type of individual. It is well known that he requires little sleep and always is looking for the next challenge. His leadership and hands-on approach contributed to the success of Microsoft and the computer software industry. His tireless efforts to advance and improve software technology and stay ahead of the competition typify the strong angular-house emphasis in his horoscope.

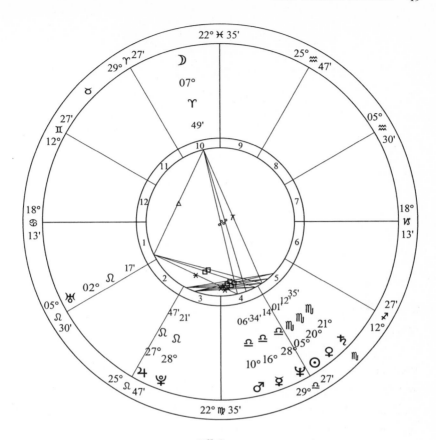

Bill Gates

October 28, 1955 / 9:15 p.m. PST / Seattle, Washington

Placidus Houses

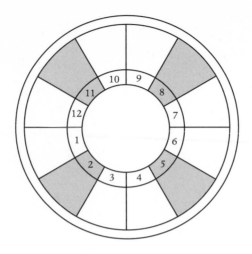

SUCCEDENT HOUSES

The succedent houses are houses 2, 5, 8, and 11. They succeed the angular houses and correspond with the fixed signs of the same number: (2) Taurus, (5) Leo, (8) Scorpio, and (11) Aquarius. These are the houses where resources are developed. They reflect what you have or hope to have. If you have a majority of planets in succedent houses, you are quite fixed in your behavior, dependable, and steady. You are focused on long-term stability and things that have lasting value. You are concerned with building substantial resources and enjoying the rewards of your efforts. Your focus is on future rather than immediate results.

A good example of emphasis in the succedent houses can be seen in the horoscope of John Fitzgerald Kennedy, the thirty-fifth president of the United States. He has six planets in succedent houses 8 and 11 and can be described as someone who had substantial resources at his disposal, both material and personal. He was a visionary who took action in the cause of equal rights and saw a better future for our country. He put programs in place that launched the country on its longest sustained expansion since World War II. He indeed was focused on the future long-term stability of our nation.

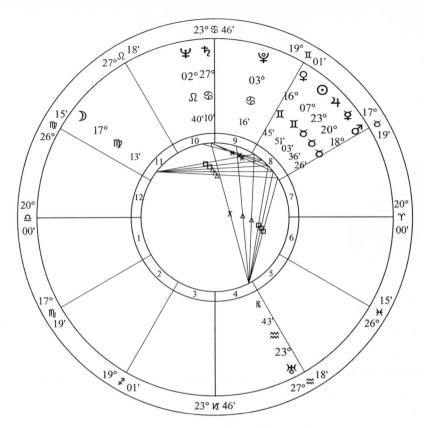

John Fitzgerald Kennedy
May 29, 1917 / 3:00 p.m. EST / Brookline, Massachusetts
Placidus Houses

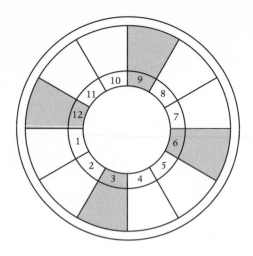

CADENT HOUSES

The cadent houses are houses 3, 6, 9, and 12. They are behind the angular houses and correspond with the mutable signs of the same number: (3) Gemini, (6) Virgo, (9) Sagittarius, and (12) Pisces. These are the houses where information is gathered and disseminated. They reflect adaptability and flexibility. If you have a majority of planets in cadent houses, you will analyze, discuss, and examine circumstances. You may be interested in research, writing, history, knowledge, or collecting data. You tend to be curious about subjects that pertain to the past, and you may disseminate information.

We have a good example of someone who embodies many of the qualities associated with the cadent houses in the horoscope of Stephen King, popular writer of horror novels. He has four planets in cadent houses 3 and 12, the houses of education, communication, and solitude. He spent his earlier years as a high school teacher of English. He began writing short stories for magazines and in the evenings worked on his novels. His horoscope's cadent-house emphasis shows his ability to spend many solitary hours researching and creating his novels.

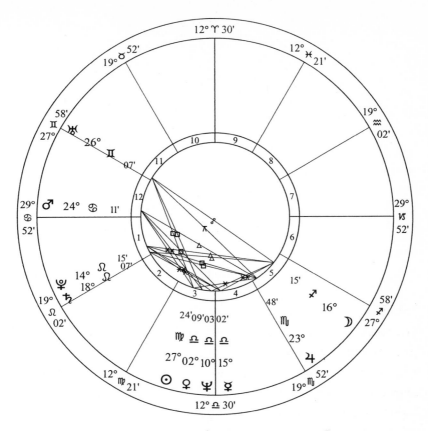

Stephen King
September 21, 1947 / 1:30 a.m. EDT / Portland, Maine
Placidus Houses

EMPTY HOUSES

Every horoscope contains some empty houses; that is to say, there are no planets residing in those houses. The only time this is significant is when you have an empty-house type—that is, if you have no planets in any of the angular, succedent, or cadent houses. Though this is rare, when it does occur, the quality associated with that empty-house type may be undefined.

The angular houses correspond with the cardinal signs. The cardinal signs take the lead; therefore, these are the houses of immediate action— where things are initiated. When there are no planets in any of the angular houses (1, 4, 7, 10), you are not so focused on the physical material world. You may be one who is idealistic, philosophical, or studious. The angular houses also are associated with the present, the here and now. A lack of planets in any angular house would suggest that you are less concerned with deeds and immediate results. Your focus will be directed toward the activities of the occupied houses in your horoscope.

The succedent houses correspond with the fixed signs. The fixed signs accumulate resources and possessions; therefore, these are the houses that show what you strive for and where you develop your resources. They are the houses associated with the future and with long-range plans. When you have no planets in any of the succedent houses (2, 5, 8, 11), it suggests that you are not very concerned with having or accumulating things. You may not be *fixated* on physical resources, but be more interested in ideas. This does not mean that you won't have material possessions; it does mean that such matters are not your primary focus in this life.

The cadent houses correspond with the mutable signs. The mutable signs are adaptable and concerned with communications; therefore, these are the houses where information is gathered and disseminated and also where work and service are performed. These are the houses associated with the past. When there are no planets in any of the cadent houses (3, 6, 9, 12), you may lack a certain curiosity or be less concerned with collecting facts and information. Studies or schooling may not be of paramount importance, and you may be uninterested in the past or what came before. There is a tendency to start things afresh regardless of past experience.

SIGNS ON THE HOUSE CUSPS

Beginning with the sign on your first-house cusp, each subsequent sign will appear on the next house cusp in order of the natural zodiac. The only exception to this is when you have an intercepted sign, and then you will see the same sign repeated on two house cusps. The sign on each house cusp describes *how* you proceed or move toward that area of life experience. These are qualities and tendencies you are in the process of developing, though they may not yet be fully realized. Every symbol in astrology—including the zodiac signs—has both positive and negative expressions. The sign on a house cusp describes how you may optimally function in that area of life, as described in the following section. These qualities are either present or emerging.

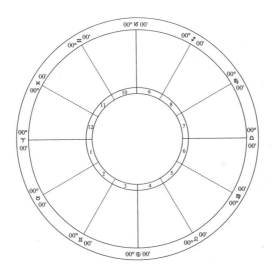

Beginning with Aries

Aries on the First-House Cusp

When Aries is on the first-house cusp we have the natural sequence of the signs on each of the subsequent house cusps and therefore what is called the natural wheel. Those with Aries on the first house are born leaders. This is the sign of self on the house of self-interest, so there is a pronounced concern with satisfying personal needs. You are a take-charge individual capable of going it alone. Assertive and fearless, you have the stamina to keep pushing until you make a breakthrough.

Taurus on the Second-House Cusp

Care and good sense are qualities you bring to the management of your personal resources with Taurus on the second-house cusp. You can accumulate assets, attract substance, and make the most of what is offered. You are practical with investments and personal income. Because you are sensible, reliable, and prudent when it comes to money, your financial future is sound.

Gemini on the Third-House Cusp

With Gemini on the third-house cusp, you are communicative and articulate. You can carry on a conversation with just about anyone. Insightful and charming, you would do well in any field that requires diplomacy or salesmanship. Your wit, perception, and good judgment make you an engaging conversationalist.

Cancer on the Fourth-House Cusp

The importance of family and tradition is apparent with Cancer on the fourth-house cusp. Your restless nature may keep you on the move, but you always return to your roots. Tradition and family are important components of your life. Your home is a place of refuge, nurturing, and support. Caring for your family and loved ones comes first no matter what your goals in life.

Leo on the Fifth-House Cusp

Vitality and self-expression are qualities you bring to your creative efforts with Leo on the fifth-house cusp. You want to be showered with love and attention and, in return, will do the same for that special someone. Children can play an important role in your life. At some point, you may enjoy recognition and honors for your creative endeavors.

Virgo on the Sixth-House Cusp

Efficiency and organization are qualities you bring to your work with Virgo on the sixth-house cusp. Your work may involve helping others. Some possible interests include health care, fitness, teaching, and counseling. Thorough and meticulous, you can sift through endless data and find solutions. You are quick to offer assistance and can work yourself ragged if the need arises.

Libra on the Seventh-House Cusp

Consideration and flexibility are qualities you bring to your relationships with Libra on the seventh-house cusp. Achieving a perfect balance with another—or as close as you can get to that ideal—is a lifelong goal. Sociable and outgoing, you can work well with the public. Your business relationships are based on mutual understanding. You seek a partner who is refined and romantic.

Scorpio on the Eighth-House Cusp

Courage and reserve are qualities you bring to shared resources with Scorpio on the eighth-house cusp. You may have an aptitude for money management, investment banking, or finance. Your own desire nature is strong, and you are passionate, secretive, and a bit mysterious about your intimacies. Loyal and discreet, you can be trusted to keep a confidence.

Sagittarius on the Ninth-House Cusp

Adventurous and open-minded describe Sagittarius on the ninth-house cusp. Your enthusiasm is catching, and you have a way of inspiring others. You may find travel—especially to foreign lands—an educational experience. Future-oriented, you are likely to explore new ideas and may introduce reform in such areas as education, religion, or the legal system.

Capricorn on the Tenth-House Cusp

Efficiency and organizational skills are qualities you bring to your career with Capricorn on the tenth-house cusp. Your work ethic, perseverance, and ambition help you make it to the top. You are capable of great strength and determination; your goals are reached through personal effort. Practical and opportunistic, you make the best of whatever comes your way.

Aquarius on the Eleventh-House Cusp

Originality and vision are qualities you bring to friendships with Aquarius on the eleventh-house cusp. You may have a diverse group of friends who are creative, inventive, or just plain eccentric. An interest in humanitarian endeavors may keep you active in the community and social groups. Your goal is to foster better understanding among those with whom you share common ground.

Pisces on the Twelfth-House Cusp

Intuition is strong with Pisces on the twelfth-house cusp. You may be able to access a wellspring of power through your connection with the universal. Gentle, compassionate, kind, and tolerant, you may feel connected with those less fortunate. This is the house of "losing oneself," and you may do so through positive or negative means.

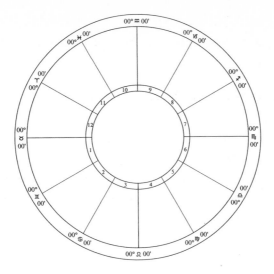

Beginning with Taurus

Taurus on the First-House Cusp

Charming, personable, and affectionate define Taurus on the first-house cusp. You are careful and deliberate, and your ability to evaluate the essence of a person makes you a good judge of character. Your persistence and patience help you stay on track until you reach your goals; no one can sway you. Not one to jump to conclusions, you are a loyal and steadfast friend.

Gemini on the Second-House Cusp

Inventiveness and versatility are qualities you bring to generating income with Gemini on the second-house cusp. You may be more interested in the creative aspects of earning a living than in the financial rewards. Your many talents enable you to do two things at once. Communication skills can play a role in making money. Broadcasting, journalism, or writing are some possibilities.

Cancer on the Third-House Cusp

Emotional, intuitive, and mentally receptive describe Cancer on the third-house cusp. You can absorb knowledge by listening and memorizing what you've heard. Your perception allows you to sense what people around you are thinking. You may change your mind many times before making a final decision, and you never forget something that has touched you emotionally.

Leo on the Fourth-House Cusp

Loyalty and generosity are at the core of your being with Leo on the fourth-house cusp. You enjoy surrounding yourself with as much luxury as you can afford and will lavish your family with the same. Your home and family are a reflection of your heritage, and you are proud of your roots. Children are likely to be an important part of your life.

Virgo on the Fifth-House Cusp

An analytical rather than emotional attitude toward matters of the heart describes Virgo on the fifth-house cusp. You may wish to maintain your independence when it comes to love. Once you make a commitment, however, your tendency toward self-sacrifice becomes evident. You're attracted to someone with whom you can exchange ideas and share long, interesting conversations.

Libra on the Sixth-House Cusp

You prefer to work in cooperation with others when Libra is on the sixth-house cusp. You or your work may gain public recognition. Your social skills and natural diplomacy are qualities you bring to your place of employment. A strong artistic inclination is likely to be expressed in your work. You may have an aptitude for drawing and design.

Scorpio on the Seventh-House Cusp

Emotional intensity and desire are qualities reflected in all partnerships—marriage and business alike—when Scorpio is on the seventh-house cusp. Your commitment to sustaining a relationship is undeniable; you are tenacious, loyal, and determined to give it your best shot. Your cunning and drive help you succeed in partnership ventures, especially when you share authority.

Sagittarius on the Eighth-House Cusp

Fairness and honesty are qualities you bring to the management of joint resources with Sagittarius on the eighth-house cusp. Your open-minded attitude about money helps attract more abundance. You have a strong inner faith coupled with curiosity about matters like death and the afterlife. Sex is of interest more as a gateway to greater awareness than mere pleasure. You can be lucky with investments.

Capricorn on the Ninth-House Cusp

Pragmatic about spiritual and philosophical matters defines Capricorn on the ninth-house cusp. You are willing to listen to new ideas but slow to embrace change. Somewhat of a purist, you may have conservative views about our educational and legal systems. Though you value a higher education, you may prefer to pursue it on your own terms and in your own time.

Aquarius on the Tenth-House Cusp

Inventiveness and imagination are qualities you bring to your career with Aquarius on the tenth-house cusp. You may excel in the scientific fields, astrology, technology, or broadcasting, but freedom of expression is important. Your reputation is often that of an eccentric genius or rabble-rouser; either way, you make a strong impression. You may challenge established ideas and traditions.

Pisces on the Eleventh-House Cusp

Supportive of and compassionate toward friends describes Pisces on the eleventh-house cusp. Your kindness and empathy endear you to many, but you can attract some who are self-destructive; know when to cut them loose. You can dream your wishes into reality if you have faith; Pisces here will dissolve barriers so you can manifest what you hope and wish for.

Aries on the Twelfth-House Cusp

Bold and fearless behind the scenes describes Aries on the twelfth-house cusp. Like the director who empowers the actor to give an excellent performance, your strength lies in helping others achieve success. Honors and recognition are bestowed when you least expect it. If faced with obstacles, you can draw on inner strength and keen intuition for guidance.

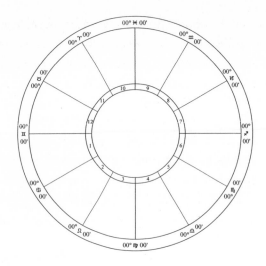

Beginning with Gemini

Gemini on the First-House Cusp

Charming, witty, and curious describe Gemini on the first-house cusp. You enjoy talking, exchanging ideas, and finding something of interest about the people you meet. If your curiosity is stirred, you have an uncanny ability to recall every bit of trivia on any subject. Your mental alertness and quick response enable you to adapt to any situation with ease.

Cancer on the Second-House Cusp

Intuition and tenacity are qualities you bring to making money with Cancer on the second-house cusp. You may generate income by way of the public and can do well in advertising, marketing, or merchandising. The food business also may provide a means of income. Generous to a fault, you are quick to share your resources with others—especially if they appeal to your emotional nature.

Leo on the Third-House Cusp

There's no limit to creative ideas with Leo on the third-house cusp. Your thoughts are original and often inspired—children of the mind, so to speak. People may find your dramatic flair entertaining, and you may choose to express yourself in writing or through the arts. You're an optimist and a true believer in the power of positive thinking.

Virgo on the Fourth-House Cusp

Everything in its place and a place for everything defines Virgo on the fourth-house cusp. Your ability to organize and multitask makes for an orderly home environment. You may choose to work from home or run a business in your home. You have an inner need to be of service, and your family and all those around you benefit from your assistance.

Libra on the Fifth-House Cusp

Consideration and compassion are qualities you bring to romance with Libra on the fifth-house cusp. Idealistic when it comes to love, you seek harmony and cohesiveness in your relationships. You think of marriage as a lifelong commitment and desire the perfect union. Your good taste and artistic appreciation are likely to be reflected in your own creative endeavors.

Scorpio on the Sixth-House Cusp

Courage and determination are qualities you bring to your work with Scorpio on the sixth-house cusp. Your work can have a cathartic effect, and you are most productive when left on your own. A strong creative bent may lead you to try many different things before you decide what you really want to do. Job interests may include police, undercover, or intelligence work or investigative research.

Sagittarius on the Seventh-House Cusp

Expansiveness, generosity, and independence are qualities you bring to your relationships with Sagittarius on the house of partners. You may need a great deal of latitude in your relationships and often prefer not to marry until late in life. If you marry, you want a partner who shares your adventures. You are happiest when you have a companion who is equally independent.

Capricorn on the Eighth-House Cusp

A conservative approach to investments describes Capricorn on the eighth-house cusp. Though you may be quite generous with your own money, your mutual assets should be handled with care. If you rely on professional investment advisors or money managers, you are likely to have better results. Though you may have anxiety about growing old, you look youthful all of your life.

Aquarius on the Ninth-House Cusp

An interest in unorthodox, inventive, or new ideas describes Aquarius on the ninth-house cusp. You may explore a philosophy or religion that is different from your own. Unusual studies like astrology or the relatively new science of quantum physics may attract your attention. You can feel at home with people of different backgrounds or cultures.

Pisces on the Tenth-House Cusp

Fantasy, imagination, and insight are qualities you bring to your career with Pisces on the tenth-house cusp. You may use creative, artistic, or musical talent in your profession. Your emotional nature plays a key role in what you do, because money alone does not make you happy. The dramatic or healing arts are possible career choices.

Aries on the Eleventh-House Cusp

Courage, bravery, and excitement are qualities you bring to friendships with Aries on the eleventh-house cusp. Your competitive spirit is admired by your friends who share your thirst for adventure. You define yourself through your friends, as they provide a sounding board for your ideas. You delight in the competition more than in the attainment of your goals.

Taurus on the Twelfth-House Cusp

A sense of insecurity where finances are concerned defines Taurus on the twelfth-house cusp. Though you are quite talented, you may not believe it and may give away your resources, both material and creative. You may utilize your many talents to help those who are less fortunate. You can tap into that wellspring within to bring your creative ideas to light.

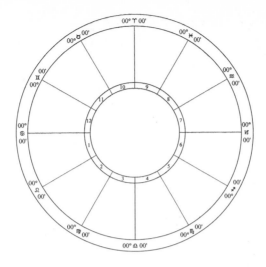

Beginning with Cancer

Cancer on the First-House Cusp

Sensitivity, intuition, and perception are qualities you exhibit in your interactions with others with Cancer on the first-house cusp. Though you love home and family, a restless nature may take you in many directions before you settle down. Interested in history and the past, you may like to collect antiques. Your caring nature helps you connect with people, and you can do well in any field that serves their needs.

Leo on the Second-House Cusp

Creativity, determination, and confidence are qualities you bring to making money with Leo on the second-house cusp. You're interested in money, not for materialistic reasons but for the sense of security it gives you. You may do well in business because you enjoy creative challenges and will take a chance with your resources. You have an aptitude for creative financing.

Virgo on the Third-House Cusp

An analytical and discriminating mind describes Virgo on the third-house cusp. You're a good listener, though you may be hesitant to express your own point of view. Your talent for detailed research may lead to a career in writing or publishing. You enjoy sharing information and knowledge and may be happy working in education or health care.

Libra on the Fourth-House Cusp

A beautiful home—one that reflects style and elegance—describes Libra on the fourth-house cusp. You may enjoy entertaining friends and having social gatherings in your home. Amicable family relationships are important, and you strive to maintain a pleasant home environment. Your artistic and creative side is likely to be reflected in your home decor. You strive for inner balance.

Scorpio on the Fifth-House Cusp

Emotional intensity and magnetism are qualities you bring to romance with Scorpio on the fifth-house cusp. You may be somewhat secretive and guarded with lovers and children unless you have cultivated the higher vibration of Scorpio. Then you are loyal, discreet, and devoted to both. Deeply aware of the power of intention, you can focus and manifest your will.

Sagittarius on the Sixth-House Cusp

Work that satisfies a sense of curiosity describes Sagittarius on the sixth-house cusp. You prefer to be on the move and would find it difficult to sit at a desk all day. Your skills are wide-ranging, and you may work well in the fields of education, travel, or publishing. Intuitive and direct, you may enjoy counseling or ministering to those in need.

Capricorn on the Seventh-House Cusp

Cautiously optimistic about marriage and relationships describes Capricorn on the seventh-house cusp. Though you may desire a committed union, you don't want to be restricted. Your preference is an unbounded relationship that gives you a sense of security without limitations. You may attract a partner who is dependable, hardworking. and ambitious.

Aquarius on the Eighth-House Cusp

Creativity, originality, and insightfulness are qualities you bring to the management of joint resources with Aquarius on the eighth-house cusp. You may have a psychic or intuitive awareness of the afterlife. Your investment strategies are quite unique and can be profitable. You are attracted to brainy types and may prefer friendship to intimacy.

Pisces on the Ninth-House Cusp

Compassion and kindness are qualities you strive for with Pisces on the ninth-house cusp. You are strongly attracted to the mystical aspects of life and may pursue a spiritual path. You covet peace of mind more than any other quality and can impart that to others. Your trusting disposition exposes you to all sorts of people, even those who are not always trustworthy.

Aries on the Tenth-House Cusp

Confidence, assertiveness, and competitiveness are qualities you bring to your career with Aries on the tenth-house cusp. You may try many different things until you find your niche; then you keep pushing until you make it. Since you like the adventure of new challenges, you would do well in a profession in which you could use your dynamic energy for change. Your leadership qualities are considerable.

Taurus on the Eleventh-House Cusp

Loyalty, patience, and dependability are qualities you bring to friendships with Taurus on the eleventh-house cusp. You seek financial independence and the status that goes with it. Though you will share your resources with a friend in need, it gives you comfort knowing you have plenty of money to go around. Persistent and steady in pursuing your goals, you're not easily deterred.

Gemini on the Twelfth-House Cusp

Intuitive gifts are enhanced with Gemini on the twelfth-house cusp. Learn to trust your instincts instead of analyzing them. You have a strong sense of duty and responsibility toward relatives. Siblings in particular can be problematic, and you may have a better relationship with them from afar. Sensitivity to surroundings affects your mood, so create a serene setting for yourself.

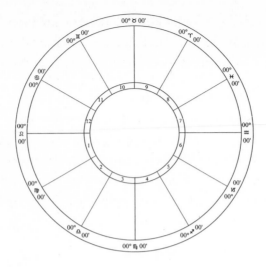

Beginning with Leo

Leo on the First-House Cusp

Idealistic, romantic, and in love with the good life describe Leo on the first-house cusp. You want to live well and will take risks to create whatever is important to your happiness. Like the Sun (the ruler of Leo), whose light and energy sustains us, you are happiest when you share your warmth with everyone. You have the ability to encourage others, and they look to you for guidance.

Virgo on the Second-House Cusp

Ready to lend a hand describes Virgo on the second-house cusp. You think of money as a means to making life easier for yourself and others. Income is generated through hard work and your own efforts. Self-reliant, you prefer not to depend on others for financial support. You are quite generous and would not hesitate to give financial assistance to someone in need.

Libra on the Third-House Cusp

A desire to please those around you describes Libra on the third-house cusp. You may go along with what others want just to keep things agreeable. You do not like to argue and will do your best to avoid confrontation, but sometimes it's preferable to take a stand on the issues. You can write about style, fashion, and artistic appreciation.

Scorpio on the Fourth-House Cusp

Inner strength and resilience describe Scorpio on the fourth-house cusp. You are devoted to your family even though the dynamics can be stressful. Your commitment to finding solutions opens the way to personal transformation. You may find it constructive and healthful to bring family secrets out in the open. You can receive financial benefits through real estate or inherited property.

Sagittarius on the Fifth-House Cusp

Enthusiastic about life, love, and romance describes Sagittarius on the fifth-house cusp. You simply like to have fun, and you're always looking for the next adventure. You are a person who doesn't mind taking risks, and you may sometimes leap before you look. But good luck saves you from the worst every time. You have wide-ranging creative interests and may travel extensively.

Capricorn on the Sixth-House Cusp

Willing to work hard well into your latter years describes Capricorn on the sixth-house cusp. Whatever work you choose, you give it your best effort. You are dependable, conscientious, and often admired by coworkers who look to you for leadership. A strong work ethic, ambition, and perseverance help you succeed in your own business.

Aquarius on the Seventh-House Cusp

With Aquarius on the seventh-house cusp, you desire a partner who is also a friend. You do well in unstructured relationships, preferring a certain amount of freedom and independence. You may attract others who are distinctive, original, and even peculiar but feel right at home because of your own uniqueness. Relationships can be problematic unless you give your partner equal autonomy.

Pisces on the Eighth-House Cusp

Powerful intuition and insight about others describe Pisces on the eighth-house cusp. You may be among those with psychic ability or the capacity to act as a medium. Caution with financial investments is advised with this placement. Money can slip right through your hands, but this can be avoided with the help of a trustworthy advisor.

Aries on the Ninth-House Cusp

Optimistic, energetic, and hopeful about life describe Aries on the ninth-house cusp. You have many new and original ideas that you can implement in whatever work you choose. Adventurous and curious about other cultures and their beliefs and lifestyles, you may decide to travel around the world. You're unafraid to try something new and always are looking for the next opportunity.

Taurus on the Tenth-House Cusp

An artistic flair, practicality, and persistence are qualities you bring to your career with Taurus on the tenth-house cusp. You have what it takes to be financially successful in your career and more so when you can delegate authority to others. Creativity will somehow be expressed in your profession or vocation, whether it is business and finance or a more artistic endeavor.

Gemini on the Eleventh-House Cusp

A genuine interest in people draws many friends with Gemini on the eleventh-house cusp. You love to exchange ideas and share information and good stories with your circle of friends. Diverse interests can make it difficult to focus on one objective at a time; you always seem to have more than one iron in the fire. Try not to spread yourself too thin.

Cancer on the Twelfth-House Cusp

Sensitivity and compassion are qualities you bring to those in need with Cancer on the twelfth-house cusp. You have a strong sense of responsibility toward family and may take care of your mother. If your feelings are hurt, you will hide it rather than talk about it. Your emotional nature is a hidden strength, especially when used to help others.

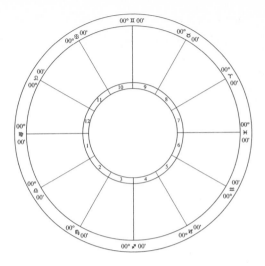

Beginning with Virgo

Virgo on the First-House Cusp

The desire to serve others describes Virgo on the first-house cusp. You maintain a youthful appearance no matter what your age. Though you are gifted and often intellectual, you may not feel a sense of power. Your work usually is done quietly behind the scenes. Detail-oriented, you are able to organize the finer points that others may find tedious. You're always looking for a way to improve something, and your analytical ability helps toward that end.

Libra on the Second-House Cusp

Social skills, charm, and finesse are qualities you bring to making money with Libra on the second-house cusp. You enjoy connecting with people and may do well in sales. Though you are fair in sharing your resources with a partner, you expect equal treatment. You have a refined way about you and dislike anything that is crude or coarse.

Scorpio on the Third-House Cusp

A probing and discriminating mind defines Scorpio on the third-house cusp. Suffice to say, you can find out anything you want to know, and uncovering information is a lifelong commitment. Your persistence makes you an excellent researcher, salesperson, or writer. Because you are somewhat secretive, others don't really know what you're thinking unless you want them to.

Sagittarius on the Fourth-House Cusp

Inner wisdom and a spiritual nature describe Sagittarius on the fourth-house cusp. Though you are reticent, if you witness injustice, you can be quite vocal in expressing your discontent. You are given to thinking about the larger issues and deeper meaning of life. In this vein, you may teach, counsel, write, or share your thoughts in other ways.

Capricorn on the Fifth-House Cusp

Shy and reserved when it comes to matters of the heart describes Capricorn on the fifth-house cusp. You may be hesitant to open yourself to love, for it's not in your nature to take risks. In romance, you prefer someone who is practical and dependable and who can provide material security. Where children are concerned, you are a good parent and role model.

Aquarius on the Sixth-House Cusp

Imagination, creativity, and originality are qualities you bring to your work with Aquarius on the sixth-house cusp. You may walk to the beat of your own drum and bring new ideas to what you do. You like a challenge in your work, and anything that is new or cutting-edge will be of interest. You may prefer alternative approaches to maintaining good health.

Pisces on the Seventh-House Cusp

With Pisces on the seventh-house cusp, you desire a partner who is sensitive, imaginative, and kind. You can attract a gentle, tolerant individual who is spiritual in nature, or someone who is secretive or deceptive. Discretion is the key with Pisces on the relationship house. Your desire to help others is commendable, but don't become a martyr.

Aries on the Eighth-House Cusp

Assertive in the handling of joint investments describes Aries on the eighth-house cusp. Your intuition coupled with keen judgment helps you make sound financial decisions. You may have an interest in helping others manage their resources. Your independent nature, however, makes it difficult for you to ask for help when needed; you prefer to go it alone.

Taurus on the Ninth-House Cusp

A steady seeker of wisdom describes Taurus on the ninth-house cusp. You are interested in any philosophy that offers harmony and equality as a precept, though you insist on practical tools. Once you make a commitment to learning all you can about a subject, nothing will sway you. You have a talent for expressing difficult concepts in a way that is easily understood—the mark of a good teacher.

Gemini on the Tenth-House Cusp

Career options are diverse with Gemini on the tenth-house cusp, as you are versatile and skilled. You may try several different things before settling on a career, but worry not—you have a wealth of talent to draw from. Strong communication skills likely will play a role in your chosen career. Writing, publishing, teaching, counseling, broadcasting, and journalism are some possibilities.

Cancer on the Eleventh-House Cusp

With Cancer on the eleventh-house cusp, you may nurture a family of friends. You are a good friend though selective about whom you take into the fold. With your strong intuition, your perceptive insights about people usually are right on the mark. Though you are receptive to new ideas, you always go with what feels right. You are tenacious in the pursuit of your hopes and wishes.

Leo on the Twelfth-House Cusp

A desire to sustain others from behind the scenes describes Leo on the twelfth-house cusp. Your light shines when you further a cause, help people, or share knowledge. You may choose to make personal sacrifices to bring your vision to the world. You prefer to remain out of the spotlight and may choose solitary work, such as research and writing. The desire to understand life's mysteries may take you on a lifelong spiritual journey.

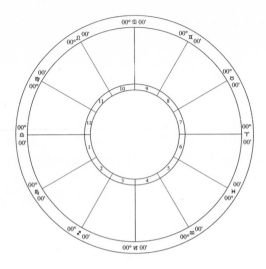

Beginning with Libra

Libra on the First-House Cusp

Fairness, diplomacy, and consideration are qualities you bring to your interactions with others with Libra on the first-house cusp. You prefer doing things with someone rather than going it alone. It may take you a while to form an opinion because you can see both sides of an issue and would rather be impartial. When you do take a stand and express your viewpoint, it is always with tact and grace.

Scorpio on the Second-House Cusp

Secretive, shrewd, and astute with money describe Scorpio on the second-house cusp. You have a good grasp of financial matters and an aptitude for investment strategies. It's likely that you will accumulate substantial assets, though you may struggle with different strategies. Later in life, you may develop a new set of values based on less materialistic goals.

Sagittarius on the Third-House Cusp

Good judgment, honesty, and candor describe Sagittarius on the third-house cusp. Interested in fair play, you may be attracted to a career in the legal profession. You always set high standards and want to discover all there is to know about a subject; you dislike being caught unprepared. Your adventurous spirit may find expression through travel or books.

Capricorn on the Fourth-House Cusp

A strong sense of responsibility toward family describes Capricorn on the fourth-house cusp. A traditionalist at heart, you want a home and family of your own and often marry early in life. You may be interested in land development and could do well buying or selling real estate. Your ambitious nature and strong work ethic enable you to succeed in business.

Aquarius on the Fifth-House Cusp

Freedom of self-expression is important with Aquarius on the fifth-house cusp. Though you are a loving and sensible person, should someone step on your creative toes, you are quick to rebel. If you have children, they are likely to be quite original, even inventive—with a strong independent streak. Your friends play an important role, and one may turn out to be the love of your life.

Pisces on the Sixth-House Cusp

Sensitivity and a willingness to serve are qualities you bring to work with Pisces on the sixth-house cusp. You may choose to work in education, health care, or another service-oriented field. Your compassionate and caring nature engenders trust from both co-workers and those you assist. You thrive when you feel you are making a contribution.

Aries on the Seventh-House Cusp

With Aries on the seventh-house cusp, you desire a partner who takes the lead and provides some direction. Though you gravitate toward relationships early on, you fare better in marriage if you wait. You like a partner who gives you a push now and then and someone you can turn to for advice. While you may be easygoing, you prefer others who challenge you.

Taurus on the Eighth-House Cusp

Prudent and hands-on when it comes to managing joint resources describe Taurus on the eighth-house cusp. Practical about money, you may be interested in a career in banking or financial services. You can accumulate your own resources by assisting others with theirs—material or spiritual. Money flows more freely when shared with your partner.

Gemini on the Ninth-House Cusp

Natural curiosity and inquisitiveness are qualities of mind with Gemini on the ninth-house cusp. Travel is an educational experience, and you enjoy learning about other people and cultures. You are just as comfortable in a foreign land as in your own backyard. You have a good grasp of the law and legal language and could be a fine attorney, judge, or court reporter.

Cancer on the Tenth-House Cusp

Intuition and public awareness are qualities you bring to your career with Cancer on the tenth-house cusp. You may pursue a career in the public arena or one in which you gauge public interest, such as marketing or advertising. Your restless nature may cause you to change careers frequently until you find something that you feel at home with. Your relationship with your mother is a key influence in your life.

Leo on the Eleventh-House Cusp

With Leo on the eleventh-house cusp, you likely have influential friends who play an important role in your life. They can open doors, but it's your sheer force of will and optimism that bring success. Once you set your sights on something, it is within your reach. Loyalty, generosity, and affection are qualities you share with friends. In a group, you can be quite entertaining and are always the center of attention.

Virgo on the Twelfth-House Cusp

Assisting others can take many forms with Virgo on the twelfth-house cusp. You may volunteer your time or collaborate with others to help a favorite charity. Or you may do work that requires a certain amount of solitude, such as writing and research. Concern about health and well-being can be allayed through service to others. You may like to work in an institutional setting.

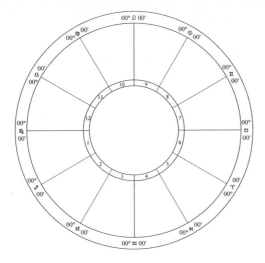

Beginning with Scorpio

Scorpio on the First-House Cusp

A quiet reserve that commands respect describes Scorpio on the first-house cusp. Others can sense your intensity even when you say nothing at all. You have great energy and remarkable determination, so once you set your sights on a goal, there's no stopping you. Nothing appeals to you more than something that is slightly out of reach. You love the challenge and rise to the occasion.

Sagittarius on the Second-House Cusp

A generous nature and desire to share what you have with others describe Sagittarius on the second-house cusp. You think of money as a means to enjoy life fully and rarely worry about not having enough. You are blessed with an inner feeling of well-being and faith that all material needs will be met. Financial risks can prove rewarding.

Capricorn on the Third-House Cusp

Serious and deliberate in gathering information describes Capricorn on the third-house cusp. You take the time to understand the issues thoroughly before offering an opinion. Your ability to think things through makes you a good strategist. Though you sometimes dwell on disappointments, your sense of humor helps you keep things in perspective.

Aquarius on the Fourth-House Cusp

Resourcefulness and creativity run deep with Aquarius on the fourth-house cusp. Your early home environment may have been chaotic, but it offered a unique setting in which to grow and mature. Humanitarian at heart, you have a strong desire to help others. You feel at home with your friends, who are usually creative, distinctive, and unconventional.

Pisces on the Fifth-House Cusp

An idealistic and even naïve view of love describes Pisces on the fifth-house cusp. You are sensitive and caring in matters of the heart and will make sacrifices for love. Learn to discriminate between those who are worthy and those who are not, lest you be disappointed. Your children may show signs of musical and artistic talent. They will be very perceptive, creative, and impressionable.

Aries on the Sixth-House Cusp

Ambition and drive to reach peak performance describe Aries on the sixth-house cusp. You have the capacity to press on long after others have grown weary. Your excellent management skills stem from a keen sense of what each person can bring to the table. You are willing to take the lead, and no challenge is too great. An interest in physical fitness may lead to work in the health care field.

Taurus on the Seventh-House Cusp

Savvy in evaluating what others have to offer describes Taurus on the seventh-house cusp. Your uncanny assessment of people is usually right on the mark. You are a loyal partner in both business and personal relationships. Your own sense of self-worth is greatly enhanced with the right partner who can bring steadiness and stability to your life.

Gemini on the Eighth-House Cusp

Curious about life's mysteries describes Gemini on the eighth-house cusp. You may be interested in psychic phenomena, astrology, or similar subjects. Your curiosity knows no bounds, taking you on many paths of exploration. You may have an aptitude for managing other's resources, personal or material. Counseling or teaching people may appeal to you.

Cancer on the Ninth-House Cusp

A highly intuitive connection with other people describes Cancer on the ninth-house cusp. You may even have prophetic dreams or impressions of forthcoming events. Instinctive about public opinion, you can sense the next hot trend or fashion. You feel at home with people from all walks of life and share a sense of belonging no matter where your travels take you.

Leo on the Tenth-House Cusp

Whatever you do attracts attention when Leo is on the tenth-house cusp. You take pride in your reputation and always put forth your best effort. Your management style radiates a sense of confidence, and those around you feel empowered by your example. A generous spirit and willingness to take others under your wing attract the admiration of your peers.

Virgo on the Eleventh-House Cusp

Always ready to help a friend in need describes Virgo on the eleventh-house cusp. Your friends are those with whom you can discuss and analyze your ideas; you share a desire to help people. You want to be of service and would be a wonderful teacher, guide, or counselor. You may have a love of animals and can be very receptive to their needs.

Libra on the Twelfth-House Cusp

Relationships demand a great deal of flexibility with Libra on the twelfth-house cusp. You may have to balance your needs with those of the other to achieve cooperation in partnerships and marriage in particular. You can work in concert with others behind the scenes. A sense of inner peace is more easily sustained in a solitary setting; you may be drawn to meditation or other spiritual practices.

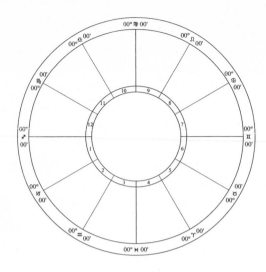

Beginning with Sagittarius

Sagittarius on the First-House Cusp

Optimism, generosity, and inspiration are qualities you bring to others with Sagittarius on the first-house cusp. Life will never be dull because you always seek the next adventure. Your search for truth may take you on a spiritual quest at some point in your life. You are a seeker of wisdom with a love of freedom and will embrace life to the fullest.

Capricorn on the Second-House Cusp

A conservative attitude regarding money and personal resources defines Capricorn on the second-house cusp. Though you have a generous spirit, you may worry needlessly about assets. Your diligence and management skills enable you to accumulate substantial reserves. You can have financial success in business and real estate.

Aquarius on the Third-House Cusp

A unique way of thinking separates you from everyone else with Aquarius on the third-house cusp. Your ideas can be innovative, original, and imaginative. Future-oriented, you are interested in everything new and cutting-edge. Creative thinking enables you to find solutions to existing problems. You are interested in the welfare of others and are willing to speak out.

Pisces on the Fourth-House Cusp

Sensitive to family needs describes Pisces on the fourth-house cusp. You may have obligations to fulfill in this area, so your tendency is to sacrifice too much. You feel a strong desire to connect with your spiritual roots. You may employ meditation, prayer, or other means to sustain that connection. Your tolerance and empathy know no bounds.

Aries on the Fifth-House Cusp

A zest for life and all that it has to offer describes Aries on the fifth-house cusp. It's in your nature to take chances, and you like anything that involves some risk. You may gamble with investments, sports, or games of chance because you like the excitement and challenge. Among your many talents is a persuasive ability; you can be a fine salesperson. You are a worthy competitor in any arena.

Taurus on the Sixth-House Cusp

Dependability, reliability, and loyalty are qualities you bring to your work with Taurus on the sixth-house cusp. As long as you love what you're doing, all is well. On the other hand, you have little tolerance for work that is not engaging. Your artistic and creative side often is expressed in what you do. A certain endurance and stamina enables you to maintain good health.

Gemini on the Seventh-House Cusp

With Gemini on the seventh-house cusp, you desire a partner who is intelligent, communicative, and flexible. If you do settle down, it is with someone who gives you plenty of freedom. A restless streak is likely to keep you on the move, and you can attract others who are equally independent. An unbounded partnership works best for you.

Cancer on the Eighth-House Cusp

An emotional, intuitive connection with others describes Cancer on the eighth-house cusp. Though you can appear detached, you are highly sensitive and may hide your feelings. But your caring nature surfaces in your intimate relationships, in which you express yourself freely. You may have premonitions or even psychic impressions about those who have passed on.

Leo on the Ninth-House Cusp

Confidence that life is meant to be good defines Leo on the ninth-house cusp. You are idealistic and believe that you can make a difference in the world. A love of travel and new horizons may beckon, and you are often on the move. You value education—whether academic, spiritual, or worldly—as a means of broadening the mind, and you enthusiastically share your wisdom with others.

Virgo on the Tenth-House Cusp

Diligence, efficiency, and benevolence are qualities you bring to your career with Virgo on the tenth-house cusp. You want to do meaningful work and can employ your fine communication skills in the fields of teaching, counseling, or public service. Your objective in life is to serve and to make a contribution. You have a reputation for honesty and integrity and enjoy the respect of your peers.

Libra on the Eleventh-House Cusp

Talented in many ways describes Libra on the eleventh-house cusp. If you're overly concerned with what others think, you can be indecisive about your goals. When you balance your needs with those of others, you make the right choices. Charming and sociable, you attract many friends, with whom you share an active social life. You may marry someone who was first a friend.

Scorpio on the Twelfth-House Cusp

Powerful hidden strengths—or weaknesses—define Scorpio on the twelfth-house cusp. The sign of death and regeneration on the house of obligations suggests that there is more work to be done in reaching your true potential. Powerful and focused, you have the capacity to help those who are less fortunate. When you set your mind on a worthy cause, you are unrelenting.

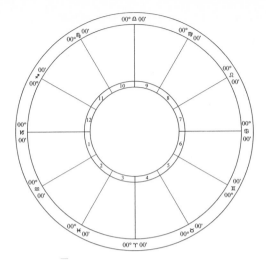

Beginning with Capricorn

Capricorn on the First-House Cusp

Determination, professionalism, and dedication are qualities you bring to others with Capricorn on the first-house cusp. Your endurance and perseverance enable you to climb to the top in whatever field you choose. You work so hard to accomplish your goals that you may not stop long enough to enjoy the rewards. Your pride and dignity command that you be treated with the respect you have earned.

Aquarius on the Second-House Cusp

Creativity and inventiveness enhance income with Aquarius on the second-house cusp. You can make good financial decisions when you listen to your instincts, but you also can be impulsive with money. Though you will accumulate assets, you may experience reversals from time to time. Worry not, for you can always land on your feet.

Pisces on the Third-House Cusp

A vivid imagination and strong intuition describe Pisces on the third-house cusp. A sensitivity of mind may be expressed through music or other creative means. You may have psychic impressions or precognitive dreams. Sometimes you may doubt yourself and even have difficulty determining what is real. You can use your talents to assist others and feel a great sense of accomplishment.

Aries on the Fourth-House Cusp

Home is the place where you reign supreme when Aries is on the fourth-house cusp. Though your home is important, you may spend little time there, as the demands of career keep you occupied. You strive to maintain a balance between family needs and career obligations. Relationships with family members are likely to be dynamic, competitive, and at times argumentative.

Taurus on the Fifth-House Cusp

Committed to creating something of value describes Taurus on the fifth-house cusp. Whether you create children of the mind or body, you give the same care, passion, and dedication to all your creative endeavors. If you do have children, you will spare no effort to provide for their needs. You are affectionate, patient, and loyal in love, though you may be possessive.

Gemini on the Sixth-House Cusp

Versatile and adaptable, you may hold two jobs when Gemini is on the sixth-house cusp. At the least, you will wear many hats in the work you do. Your state of mind has an effect on your health because you tend to worry too much. You may be self-critical and somewhat of a perfectionist. You can learn relaxation techniques, which will be quite helpful to your well-being.

Cancer on the Seventh-House Cusp

Nurturing, maternal, and accommodating are qualities you bring to your relationships with Cancer on the seventh-house cusp. You prefer a partner who loves home, family, and tradition. Receptive to public opinion, you have an instinctive feel for what is trendy, popular, or in vogue. You may be drawn to a career in the public arena or gain public recognition for your efforts.

Leo on the Eighth-House Cusp

Sharing the spotlight with partners and people in general describes Leo on the eighth-house cusp. You have a knack for assessing others' talents. This makes for a good administrator, capable of delegating and bringing the right people together. A creative approach to investments and money management helps you succeed with financial endeavors.

Virgo on the Ninth-House Cusp

Understanding the finer points of broader concepts defines Virgo on the ninth-house cusp. You have a knack for simplifying complex ideas and can point the way for others. You may be an excellent teacher, counselor, or manager. Travel for business or work-related matters is likely. When you're curious about something, you learn all you can and become an expert of sorts.

Libra on the Tenth-House Cusp

Style, diplomacy, and fairness are qualities you bring to your career with Libra on the tenth-house cusp. You are seen as a person who is just and equitable in your business dealings. Your natural charm and public appeal would support a high-profile career. You may be drawn to politics, law, or administration. You have the capacity to attract people who will assist you in accomplishing your goals.

Scorpio on the Eleventh-House Cusp

Tenacity, assertiveness, and discrimination are qualities you bring to friendships with Scorpio on the eleventh-house cusp. You may attract powerful friends, though you are cautious and somewhat reluctant to share your ideas with them until they have gained your trust. Though you like the public arena, in your private life you are more of a loner and prefer the company of a few good friends.

Sagittarius on the Twelfth-House Cusp

With Sagittarius on the twelfth-house cusp, you have faith in a higher power that sustains life. Inner strength and optimism guide you through life's challenges. Though material success is important, you may feel burdened with the need to sustain it. You often are happiest when you can set aside your ambitions and focus on life's simple joys.

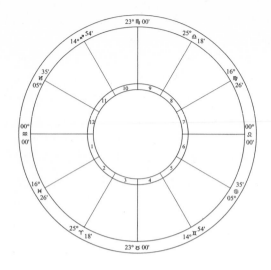

Beginning with Aquarius

Aquarius on the First-House Cusp

Friendly and outgoing, with a touch of eccentricity, describe Aquarius on the first-house cusp. Your love of freedom keeps you from doing anything that infringes on that. Strongly independent, you follow your own counsel and hardly care what others think. You enjoy helping people, and at some point your life may take an unexpected turn in a new direction.

Pisces on the Second-House Cusp

Generous with material resources describes Pisces on the second-house cusp. Your income may be derived from a creative endeavor, such as music, or service, such as nursing. You are sensitive to the needs of others and may give some of your personal assets to support those who are less fortunate. Your values are more clearly defined when you mingle and work with others.

Aries on the Third-House Cusp

A desire to seek new knowledge describes Aries on the third-house cusp. You have strong opinions and convictions, though you welcome a good debate. You're not afraid to think outside the box or to implement new ideas. With a dynamic way of speaking, you may do well in sales, promotion, or public speaking. You have a pioneering spirit and are a force to be reckoned with.

Taurus on the Fourth-House Cusp

A beautiful home and lovely possessions describe Taurus on the fourth-house cusp; your home may be a showcase for your collections. You enjoy what money can buy, and the accumulation of substance gives you a sense of well-being. You can make money with real estate. Conservative when it comes to family matters, you are a loyal and devoted parent.

Gemini on the Fifth-House Cusp

An intellectual approach to matters of the heart defines Gemini on the fifth-house cusp. You can fall in love with someone's mind and quickly lose interest if communication is lacking; on the other hand, with a good sense of humor, love blossoms. You are versatile and talented in many ways, and your words may be published. If you have children, they, too, are likely to be multitalented.

Cancer on the Sixth-House Cusp

Kindness, loyalty, and intuition are qualities you bring to your work with Cancer on the sixth-house cusp. It is easier for you to express your feelings through your work than in other areas of your life. Your work may involve the food business, the public, or children. Adaptable and intuitive, you are able to change direction when needed and stay ahead of the trend.

Leo on the Seventh-House Cusp

Partners tend to steal the spotlight with Leo on the seventh-house cusp. In your relationships, you want someone who will give you plenty of leeway to express your individuality. You are attracted to those in a position of power who will not play a subordinate role. Others see you as a fun-loving, generous, and creative person who is always the life of the party.

Virgo on the Eighth-House Cusp

An ability to analyze the best course of action describes Virgo on the eighth-house cusp. Your good judgment and insight are sought by those who value your counsel. Good at managing other people's resources, you can improve and streamline operations. You are at your best when offering help to people; this may take the form of health-related services.

Libra on the Ninth-House Cusp

Open to broader concepts describes Libra on the ninth-house cusp. You may enjoy traveling and meeting people of different backgrounds. Your sense of fairness and equality may find expression through the study of law or in the diplomatic field. Your highest ideals center on justice, fairness, and a desire to find a balance between old and new ideas.

Scorpio on the Tenth-House Cusp

A powerful drive to succeed describes Scorpio on the tenth-house cusp. Ambition and sheer determination help you achieve your desired career goals. You are drawn to positions of power and would do well in your own business or the medical field, investigation and research, administration, and government. You can be recognized for your contributions and acknowledged by your peers.

Sagittarius on the Eleventh-House Cusp

An attitude of expectation describes Sagittarius on the eleventh-house cusp. Because you anticipate only the best, your dreams have a way of coming true. A genuine humanitarian, you gain many friends and can accomplish a great deal through organizational work. Your tireless energy brings people far and wide to your cause.

Capricorn on the Twelfth-House Cusp

A sense of responsibility toward those in need describes Capricorn on the twelfth-house cusp. You may care for a parent, family member, or people who cannot care for themselves. Solitary work may be of interest. Your accomplishments bring you a sense of satisfaction, especially when others benefit from your efforts. You can be honored for your efforts on behalf of others.

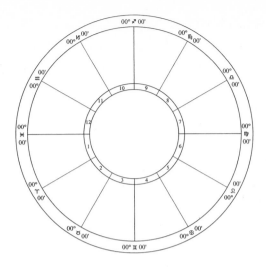

Beginning with Pisces

Pisces on the First-House Cusp

Compassion, kindness, and tolerance are qualities you bring to others with Pisces on the first-house cusp. Your intuition and psychic sensitivity are natural gifts, and you may use these talents to help people. Music, nature, and seclusion can restore your vitality. You dream big dreams but may lack the confidence to reach for them. Self-belief is the key to getting what you want.

Aries on the Second-House Cusp

A drive to succeed in the material world describes Aries on the second-house cusp. You are never quite satisfied with your financial status and are always reaching for more. Somewhat impulsive with money, you enjoy spending it and may find it hard to hold on to. But you are pretty good at creating financial opportunities and are not afraid to take risks. Timing plays a role in financial success.

Taurus on the Third-House Cusp

Creative interests and mental fortitude describe Taurus on the third-house cusp. Though you are flexible by nature, once you set your mind on something, you won't allow anything to stand in your way. Your resolve is admirable. You are thoughtful and kind in manner and rarely get angry without provocation. You may have a strong interest in music and art.

Gemini on the Fourth-House Cusp

The world is your home with Gemini on the fourth-house cusp. You may prefer to live in a large city or urban center that offers a variety of interests. While you can be friendly and sociable, there are times when you prefer the privacy and solitude of a quiet country setting. You cherish your freedom to come and go; those close to you would do well to allow it.

Cancer on the Fifth-House Cusp

Sensitive and receptive to loved ones describes Cancer on the fifth-house cusp. You want to take care of those close to you and may assume a parental role in your romantic relationships. Blessed with a fine memory and vivid imagination, you may find acting a satisfying art form. Your maternal instincts can find expression in parenting or caring for children other than your own.

Leo on the Sixth-House Cusp

The focus of life is work with Leo on the sixth-house cusp. It's very important that you love what you do, because you will devote much of your time to your work. You can feel a sense of confidence and assuredness in your occupation that may be lacking in other areas of your life. Creativity flourishes in your line of work, giving you a sense of satisfaction.

Virgo on the Seventh-House Cusp

Honesty, kindness, and thoughtfulness are qualities you bring to relationships with Virgo on the seventh-house cusp. Your desire to be of help may find expression through community service. You can become involved in defending the rights of others. In relationships, you can attract a partner who is equally civic-minded. You fare better with someone who shares your desire to help people.

Libra on the Eighth-House Cusp

An equitable handling of partnership funds describes Libra on the eighth-house cusp. Your flexibility enables you to work well with others and realize profits from partnership ventures. You may invest in municipal bonds, utilities, or other public service companies. You are likely to share financial responsibilities with your spouse or significant other.

Scorpio on the Ninth-House Cusp

A quest for deeper understanding describes Scorpio on the ninth-house cusp. You may be interested in studying philosophy, religion, or spiritual disciplines. You also can be drawn to mystery teachings and unorthodox studies. Travel and exploration can revitalize you in ways that few other things can. You have a discriminating mind and are tenacious in your pursuit of knowledge.

Sagittarius on the Tenth-House Cusp

High moral principles, generosity, and confidence are qualities you bring to your career with Sagittarius on the tenth-house cusp. You may counsel or minister to others; a career in education or the legal field is possible. Your honesty and forthrightness are admired by your peers. Open-minded and progressive, you may set new precedents in your chosen profession.

Capricorn on the Eleventh-House Cusp

Commitment and determination are qualities you bring to attaining your goals with Capricorn on the eleventh-house cusp. Your willingness to work hard and stay the course helps you reach your dreams. You prefer the company of a few good friends and may be uncomfortable with large groups of people. Friendships can carry with them some obligation or duty, though it goes both ways.

Aquarius on the Twelfth-House Cusp

Flashes of insight awaken your consciousness with Aquarius on the twelfth-house cusp. Your keen intuition enables you to sense things that sometimes are difficult to explain. You may express your originality and imagination through art, music, or other creative outlets. Gentle in nature and kind at heart, you will do anything to help a friend.

chapter five

THE PLANETS

The planets are the focal points of the horoscope. Everything manifests through the planets, though their influence is modified by the sign and house they occupy and the aspects they make. There are ten planets, or more correctly eight planets plus the Sun and Moon, which are luminaries. Each planet has a specific function and related meanings.

SUN ☉

The Sun defines your basic character, self-expression, and self-image; vital life force and physical strength; willpower and the urge for power; pride and self-esteem; individuality and creativity; conscious identity; men in general; authoritative people and officials; and dignitaries and those in power.

The Sun rules the sign of Leo ♌. It describes what you are at heart. It is the primary expression of self or will and your conscious sense of identity.

MOON ☽

The Moon defines your feelings and emotions; instinct and intuition; memory and imagination; habits and repetitive patterns; your home and family; your mother and motherhood; females in general; emotional responses; moods and manias; your ability to adapt and change; receptivity and sensitivity; and heredity and tradition.

The Moon rules the sign of Cancer ♋. It describes your instinctive responses, habits, mannerisms, and emotional makeup.

MERCURY ☿

Mercury defines your intellect and intelligence; your ability to think, gather information, and communicate; mental concentration, focus, and perception; speaking and writing; primary education; contracts and agreements; brothers and sisters; short journeys; work and co-workers; and neighborhood and surroundings.

Mercury rules both the signs of Gemini ♊ and Virgo ♍. It defines your thinking process and mental faculties. It shows your work and working environment.

VENUS ♀

Venus defines what you love; partnerships and marriage; what you attract and appreciate; money and possessions; values and principles; social, creative, and artistic interests; personal talents and abilities; material resources and valuables; one-on-one relationships; your style and social graces; and females in general.

Venus rules both the signs of Taurus ♉ and Libra ♎. It shows your ability to express affection and what you love. It also shows your money, resources, and earning capacity.

MARS ♂

Mars defines your physical energy and actions; your sense of adventure; aggressive and assertive behavior; activity in general; initiative and drive; courage, strength, and confidence; passion and zeal; combativeness and competitiveness; struggle, strife, anger, and violence; and impatience and hastiness.

Mars rules the sign of Aries ♈. It defines your actions and your sense of adventure. It shows your desire nature, sexual urges, and physical energy.

JUPITER ♃

Jupiter defines your understanding of broader concepts; principles of expansion and growth; advancement and progress; that which inspires; prosperity and abundance; optimism and joy; faith and spirituality; opportunity and good luck; curiosity; generosity and honesty; and religious and philosophical thought.

Jupiter rules the sign of Sagittarius ♐. It shows increase and expansion on a personal or material level. It defines your capacity to see the big picture.

SATURN ♄

Saturn defines your ambitions and goals; career and profession; long-term objectives; practical and material achievements; wisdom through experience; men in general; your father; superiors and authority figures; organizational ability; fears and concerns; obstacles to overcome; delays and limitations; and safety and security needs.

Saturn rules the sign of Capricorn ♑. It shows responsibilities, obligations, and recognition earned through acceptance of same.

URANUS ♅

Uranus defines originality and genius; your drive for freedom and independence; progressive and innovative thinking; individuality and vision; humanity and idealism; insight and imagination; rebelliousness and eccentricity; sudden and dramatic changes; unpredictable and unexplained events; and radical and impulsive behavior.

Uranus rules the sign of Aquarius ♒. It defines your desire for freedom, creativity, and independence. It shows unexpected and often disruptive changes.

NEPTUNE ♆

Neptune defines your imagination and perception; illusions and delusions; obligations and sacrifices; sensitivity and psychic impressions; mystical tendencies; your compassion, tolerance, and patience; musical and creative gifts; your willingness to surrender; reclusive or secretive behavior; and self-destructive behavior.

Neptune rules the sign of Pisces ♓. It defines your impractical side but also compassion and humanity. It shows idealism, sacrifice, and selfless behavior.

PLUTO ♇

Pluto defines the regenerative process; shedding and renewal; the death and rebirth of anything; sex and sexual tendencies; aggressive and extreme behavior; power and control issues; persuasive influences; courage and determination; explosive and unstable actions; and your ability to transcend adversity and free yourself.

Pluto rules the sign of Scorpio ♏. It defines your sense of power and influence. It shows resilience, renewal, and resurrection. Though astronomically Pluto has been reclassified as a dwarf planet, its astrological definition remains unchanged.

PLANETS IN THE HOUSES

In this symbolic language of astrology, the planets represent the forces within you that shape all things. Each one has a specific function and a particular operating energy. The planet defines *what* is happening in the house in which it resides. Each house of the birth chart represents a different area of life experience. It is the arena in which we express the various activities symbolized by the planets.

The following section illustrates the ways in which a planet can operate in each house. A planet often is not alone in a house. It may reside with one or more other planets in the same house, each one adding its unique energy. For example, if Mars were in the first house all by itself, we might say you have an assertive and confrontational personality. But if Venus was also there, it would soften the assertiveness of Mars and add warmth and charm to the mix; we might say you are quick to offer your help to another. Keep in mind that the horoscope—like the individual it defines—is an intricate, multifaceted combination of many different elements.

Planets in the First House

The first house defines your appearance, attitude, mannerisms, demeanor, and disposition. It shows your personality, temperament, and exterior façade, plus your physical body and the way you carry yourself. When others meet you for the first time, it is the first house that defines what they see. Any planet in the first house will give you the traits of that planet and the sign it rules.

Sun in the First House

Bold, confident, dignified, and proud—the traits of Leo are strong when the Sun is in the first house. You want to be in a position of power and are happy when you are the center of attention. Your self-expression and individuality are strong components of your personality. You exhibit warmth, courage, enthusiasm, and a zest for life. An air of authority commands respect.

Moon in the First House

Kind, emotional, maternal, and nurturing—the traits of Cancer are strong when the Moon is in the first house. You have a strong desire to please and need to feel appreciated. Your sensitivity to people makes it difficult to separate your desires from theirs. Your feelings always determine your course of action, though you may overreact at times. You may have to learn to withhold some of yourself and not give away too much.

Mercury in the First House

Curious, analytical, talented, and observant—the traits of Gemini and secondarily Virgo are strong when Mercury is in the first house. You are intellectual and have a voracious appetite for information of all kinds. Your restless nature keeps you on the go, and it's hard for you to relax. You have a tendency to overanalyze everything and worry too much. You can benefit from meditation and other techniques that help quiet the mind.

Venus in the First House

Considerate, romantic, charming, talented, and agreeable—the traits of Libra and secondarily Taurus are strong when Venus is in the first house. Your grace and elegance are reflected in your appearance, and you surround yourself with beautiful things. Friendly, outgoing, and fun-loving, you always put your best foot forward and try to cultivate cohesive relationships. You enjoy the good things life has to offer.

Mars in the First House

Confident, energetic, active, and bold—the traits of Aries are strong when Mars is in the first house. Your leadership qualities and positive attitude help you find the best way to get the job done. You are always more comfortable giving the orders and find it hard to be told what to do. Courageous and assertive, you are not afraid to take the risks necessary to achieve results. You may be argumentative when challenged, particularly in your early years.

Jupiter in the First House

Adventurous, inquisitive, open-minded, and generous—the traits of Sagittarius are strong when Jupiter is in the first house. You love your freedom and enjoy exploring new horizons. You're interested in learning and experiencing all you can about many different subjects. You enjoy the good life and may have a tendency to put on weight. Straight talk can sometimes get you in trouble, and you may have to work on being more tactful.

Saturn in the First House

Ambitious, dependable, efficient, and capable—the traits of Capricorn are strong when Saturn is in the first house. Though you are disciplined and hardworking, you may be apprehensive about achieving your objectives. However, when you focus on a goal, your perseverance, self-control, and determination result in success. You are usually mature beyond your years but maintain a youthful attitude through old age.

Uranus in the First House

Original, inventive, unusual, and eccentric—the traits of Aquarius are strong when Uranus is in the first house. You will walk your own path, explore, investigate, and break down barriers regardless of what people think. Your individuality is evident in everything you do, but you're often misunderstood. You can be impulsive or rebellious but are never boring. You are compelled to follow your powerful intuition, regardless of the outcome.

Neptune in the First House

Compassionate, tolerant, imaginative, and intuitive—the traits of Pisces are strong when Neptune is in the first house. Your sensitivity to your environment and to people may cause you to feel overwhelmed at times. You can benefit greatly from music, seclusion, and quiet contemplation. Your sympathetic nature compels you to help those in need, but don't be a martyr. You may be too trusting and idealistic; try to be grounded in reality.

Pluto in the First House

Powerful, intense, penetrating, and secretive—the traits of Scorpio are strong when Pluto is in the first house. You have a commanding presence, and people tend to follow your lead. Your intuition is so strong that you can assess any situation accurately. You have a strong healing quality both in your physical body and in the capacity to help others. You can get what you want, so be careful what you ask for; there are immediate consequences for bad behavior.

Planets in the Second House

The second house describes your money, assets, earnings, and earning capacity. It shows your material possessions such as jewelry, art, stocks, and bonds. It defines your spending habits, purchasing power, personal debts, personal resources, and financial affairs in general. It also describes your self-worth and values. Any planet in the second house influences your principles and attitude toward money.

Sun in the Second House

Self-esteem and confidence are tied to money and personal resources when the Sun is in the second house. You have a strong desire for material possessions and equate success with the accumulation of assets, substance, and material goods. Your persistence and drive help you reach financial independence. You value high standards and admire those who do not compromise their principles. You may show your affection by giving gifts.

Moon in the Second House

Financial conditions are continually changing when the Moon is in the second house. Get in the habit of building a reserve to fall back on. You may earn money in the public arena, buying and selling real estate, or in the food business. Emotional well-being is tied to the accumulation of money and assets. Your strong instincts help guide you toward sound financial investments. Receptive to current trends, you may do well in advertising or marketing.

Mercury in the Second House

Financial well-being goes hand in hand with strong communication skills when Mercury is in the second house. You may earn a living in sales, writing, public speaking, or teaching. Your primary focus is on making money, and your versatility and adaptability open many doors to that end. Worry about economic security can get out of hand if you don't keep busy. You have many good ideas about how to improve your financial stability.

Venus in the Second House

Financial benefits are easily attracted when Venus is in the second house. You desire and admire things of beauty and will accumulate lovely possessions. You may earn a living using your creative or artistic skills. Your talents extend to economic areas, and you have a practical approach to investment. You prefer quality over quantity and purchase only the best money can buy. You love to give and receive beautiful and expensive gifts.

Mars in the Second House

Money is earned directly through personal efforts, deeds, and actions when Mars is in the second house. You can generate income but may have difficulty holding on to money. Impulsive spending may play a part in monetary fluctuations. You may earn a living in the military, in engineering, or working with machinery. Your competitive drive ensures financial opportunities of your own making. You may have to learn to use your resources in a more equitable way.

Jupiter in the Second House

An optimistic outlook seems to attract money when Jupiter is in the second house. Your carefree attitude about money stems from a certain amount of luck where resources are concerned. This is not to say that you will be rich—on the contrary. You are rather unconcerned about material assets but somehow always seem to have what you need. You are more concerned with expanding your principles than your pocketbook, and you are generous with what you have. You may earn a living in sales or the travel business.

Saturn in the Second House

Financial independence and security needs are the motivating forces when Saturn is in the second house. You work very hard to ensure your financial future and often become wealthy in the process. You may have concerns that your material resources are limited and overcompensate by working all the time. An attitude of sharing what you have with others brings even more abundance. You may earn a living through real estate, construction, or land development.

Uranus in the Second House

Interruption in the flow of income, different sources of income, or income generated in unique ways describe Uranus in the second house. Your financial independence often depends on self-employment or an entrepreneurial endeavor. You are not one to be bound to routine. Imagination, creativity, and inventiveness play a key role in creating material security. You can earn a living in electronics or the field of technology.

Neptune in the Second House

Idealistic and not very practical about money describe Neptune in the second house. Your assets can seem to dissipate unless they are kept fluid. You may prefer to have someone else handle your money to better amass material wealth. Your financial security may be tied to a vocation that helps people, such as social services, teaching, or medicine. Your imagination, creativity, and intuition play a key role in creating material resources. You may earn a living in music or the arts.

Pluto in the Second House

Money for the sake of power defines Pluto in the second house; many very wealthy people have this placement. You are not half-hearted when it comes to generating income and will take an all-or-nothing approach to building material security. Financial investments are usually quite profitable because you have a strong sense of what works; you can stay ahead of changing trends. You can accumulate assets by keeping your money working rather than idle.

Planets in the Third House

The third house describes your way of communicating thoughts and ideas. It shows your mental focus, decisions, and written words. It further defines your everyday environment, like neighborhood and neighbors. It shows your siblings and your relationships with them. Short-distance travel—usually by automobile, bus, rail, or other ground vehicle—also is shown in the third house.

Sun in the Third House

Great interest in communicating thoughts and ideas through speech or the written word describes the Sun in the third house. You may have an aptitude for teaching and working with young children. Your ideas are often met with enthusiasm, and you can express yourself in a number of creative ways. Relationships with siblings are loving, and you are likely to have a strong bond with one in particular.

Moon in the Third House

Emotional sensitivity is easily conveyed when the Moon is in the third house. You have an ability to put into words both your own feelings and those of people around you. Your intuitive mind is sensitive to current trends and public opinion. You may be drawn to journalism or another form of social commentary. You tend to learn by observation and absorb knowledge like a sponge. You may change your way of thinking on many issues over your lifetime.

Mercury in the Third House

At home in the house it rules, Mercury shows an analytical mind focused on information of all sorts. Your curiosity may be concentrated on research or investigative or diagnostic work. Gathering and conveying facts and data comes easily, and you are likely to have strong verbal skills. You may be drawn to writing or reporting. Relationships with siblings and relatives usually are agreeable, though you worry about their welfare.

Venus in the Third House

An artistic and creative mind describes Venus in the third house. Your charming personality and friendly manner easily attract opportunities and new acquaintances. Interested in quality and beauty, you may be drawn to a vocation in one of the creative fields, like architecture, fashion design, or interior design. You surround yourself with lovely things that reflect your good taste. People see you as poised, elegant, and refined.

Mars in the Third House

An active mind and a straightforward way of speaking describe Mars in the third house. You are not one to mince words, though it can get you into trouble at times. Your mind is restless, and you are always anxious to get on to the next project. At times, you can be impulsive, but your strategy is usually successful. You are a good debater and welcome an exchange of ideas. Relationships with siblings can be challenging or at least competitive.

Jupiter in the Third House

An open mind, tolerance, and honesty define Jupiter in the third house. You can inspire others with your wide-ranging views on many subjects. An expansive way of thinking enables you to see the big picture and find solutions to problems. You like to understand all sides of an issue before offering an opinion; your fairness is admirable. Outspoken and candid, you sometimes give away too much information.

Saturn in the Third House

A serious, focused mind and a person who prefers to speak only when spoken to describe Saturn in the third house. Not one to make snap judgments, you take your time and gather the facts before offering an opinion. You are on a serious quest for knowledge and can be self-taught. Your integrity and fairness gain the respect of those around you. Relationships with siblings and relatives can be overbearing; you may not feel a strong connection to them.

Uranus in the Third House

An inventive and often ingenious way of thinking describes Uranus in the third house. Your creative ideas are visionary, and people see you as futuristic. Flashes of insight often reveal solutions to problems or give you new understanding. You may have an interest in science, cutting-edge technology, astrology, or other creative subjects. At times, your original ideas can meet with resistance or even shock people. Relationships with siblings can be more like friendships or somewhat unusual.

Neptune in the Third House

An imaginative mind able to create beautiful mental imagery defines Neptune in the third house. You are gentle in manner and may express yourself through musical or artistic channels. Not one to approach things by sheer logic, you follow your intuition, which guides you to the right answers. Early schooling can feel confining because you would much rather be dreaming your wonderful dreams. It's difficult for you to concentrate on anything that does not hold interest.

Pluto in the Third House

A persuasive power to communicate thoughts and ideas defines Pluto in the third house. You may impress your views on others and influence the majority. Your incisive mind lets you see beneath the surface and understand at a deeper level. When you focus, you can find the solution to any problem. Your words have a strong effect on people, and you can coax, persuade, or win them over. You can be an excellent counselor, therapist, analyst, investigator, or salesperson.

Planets in the Fourth House

The fourth house describes your home and early environment. It shows family influences and domestic affairs. It defines a parent, usually the one of lesser influence. It shows your inner self or who you are at the roots of your being. The fourth house further depicts the latter part of life. Both the sign on its cusp and any planet in this house will reflect what you become as you age.

Sun in the Fourth House

A beautiful home and one in which you are the matriarch or patriarch best describe the Sun in the fourth house. There is a strong emotional tie to home and family, though this may not be apparent on the surface. You can acquire assets, real estate, land, or buildings as a means of sustaining family affluence. Proud and loyal, you take satisfaction in caring for those family members who may need your help. As you grow older, the generosity you showed to others is returned tenfold.

Moon in the Fourth House

Shifting circumstances in the home environment describes the Moon in the fourth house. Perhaps one of your parents was an emotional person whose strong influence deeply affected you. Your home will always be a place of refuge where you find the peace and tranquility you crave. Acutely sensitive to the needs of family, you may be willing to sacrifice a lot to take care of them. You instinctively know how to please people, and you can sense public opinion.

Mercury in the Fourth House

A lively home where people exchange information and ideas describes Mercury in the fourth house. Your surroundings reflect your diverse interests, including a fine collection of books. You may work from home or have an office in your home with all the necessary equipment to run a business. You can worry excessively about family matters or change residences multiple times. As you grow older, you may be inclined to write your memoirs.

Venus in the Fourth House

Family relationships on the whole are very harmonious when Venus is in the fourth house. You have a loving bond with your parents and those you live with. Your home is likely to reflect the many creative talents you possess and be a showcase for your beautiful collections. You have a natural feel for and can earn money from interior design, decorating, or real estate investment. Your retirement years will be carefree and filled with many fun things to do.

Mars in the Fourth House

A competitive home environment or one in which there is an active, spirited exchange describes Mars in the fourth house. Without restraint, dynamic family relationships can turn argumentative. Your home is where you want to be in charge or at least independent. Your quest for inner tranquility may continue throughout your life. You will never age before your time and will be going strong long after most people grow old.

Jupiter in the Fourth House

A happy home and a free spirit describe Jupiter in the fourth house. Your sense of adventure may take you on many journeys, and you will call the world your home. Spacious and grand, your home is a reflection of your inner sense of well-being. Your early environment and upbringing have given you a joy for life. Generous by nature, your family imparted both material and spiritual values. The latter part of your life holds many blessings.

Saturn in the Fourth House

Obligations to home and family are taken seriously when Saturn is in the fourth house. One of your parents may have been absent or unavailable when you were a youngster. You have a strong sense of responsibility toward your own family and will work hard to ensure a stable, permanent home of your own. Though you may rule the roost, other family members may want autonomy. Staying busy in your latter years will keep you going for a long time.

Uranus in the Fourth House

An unusual or unconventional home, such as living on a houseboat or in an unsettling domestic environment, describes Uranus in the fourth house. Your relationship with one of your parents may have been difficult. You are unlikely to settle down in a conventional manner and may be inclined to move around a lot. Your unique perspective stems from independence gained at an early age. As you grow older, you are more comfortable expressing your special point of view.

Neptune in the Fourth House

Appearances can be deceiving and family relationships are not what they seem with Neptune in the fourth house. Your inner sensitivity and compassion are evident in the sacrifices you make for family members.

You may feel isolated from the rest of your family or mystified by the differences between you. One of your parents may be a highly sensitive, creative person or self-destructive. As you grow older, you may be drawn to assist others.

Pluto in the Fourth House

A home and family setting that is somewhat mysterious or secretive describes Pluto in the fourth house. Certain family matters can be concealed or withheld from you. An emotional, intense relationship with one of your parents may be a challenge, though there is a strong bond between you. Property or real estate can be inherited, bequeathed, or put in a trust for you. In the latter part of your life, you may experience a renaissance few others have the fortune of knowing.

Planets in the Fifth House

The fifth house defines all your creative endeavors, including children, as well as artistically inspired activities such as composing, painting, or sculpting. It shows love and romance, but not marriage (that's shown in the seventh house). It further defines all the things you do for fun—your hobbies, pastimes, enjoyments, and entertainment. Risk taking also is shown here, including gambling and speculation.

Sun in the Fifth House

Self-expression and creativity are strong when the Sun is in the fifth house, its natural domain. Your many talents distinguish you from others; you can create something that is uniquely identified with you. You will follow your heart no matter where it takes you. An optimistic attitude coupled with a willingness to take risks can help you succeed with speculation or games of chance. You certainly know how to have fun and enjoy taking others along.

Moon in the Fifth House

An emotional attachment to children and all those you love defines the Moon in the fifth house. You may feel overwhelmed at times and withdraw into a shell to protect your feelings. In romantic relationships, you are nurturing and protective; you also can attract someone who wants to take care of you. You can express yourself through artistic channels or a favorite hobby. Though shy about your talents, you adore being recognized as the creative person you are.

Mercury in the Fifth House

Creative expression through writing and speaking describes Mercury in the fifth house. You may author a book, screenplay, or script. Good communication in your romantic relationships is a must. You prefer the intelligent, witty, expressive type with whom you can share many different interests. Your children can be a handful—inquisitive, talented, and curious about everything. The more you teach them, the better; you worry needlessly about their well-being.

Venus in the Fifth House

Romantic relationships are satisfying and usually are a primary focus when Venus is in the fifth house. You are lucky in love and also with speculation. In a romantic partner, you want someone who is refined and charming. Financial gain is possible through creative endeavors such as music, art, or jewelry design, as well as speculative ventures like stock trading or the futures market. If you have children, they will be talented, charming, and caring.

Mars in the Fifth House

A great deal of creative energy can be expressed through physical activity when Mars is in the fifth house. You may have the aptitude to become a fine athlete. Your endurance, stamina, and energy may find expression through sports, competitive games, or similar activities. In the romantic department, you can be impulsive, generating lots of activity in that area. You like to take risks and may enjoy gambling. Your children may be hyper and need to be kept busy.

Jupiter in the Fifth House

Confident in your ability to be creative describes Jupiter in the fifth house. You are blessed with many talents and artistic gifts, but you also have the good fortune to attract financial backing. Belief in yourself plus an optimistic nature helps you win at almost anything you try. Inspired by a rich imagination, you never lack ideas for your next project. Your kind and giving nature attracts many love interests. You can have financial gain through your children (of body or mind) and through speculation.

Saturn in the Fifth House

A creative project that withstands the test of time describes Saturn in the fifth house. Though it may take you time, you have the perseverance to bring your ideas to fruition. Your sense of self can be somewhat diminished, so you may lack confidence in your talents. In romantic relationships, you strive to express your feelings, though this does not come easily. You may fall in love with someone who is much older or much younger; in any case, love may arrive later in life.

Uranus in the Fifth House

An inventive streak expressed through your creative endeavors describes Uranus in the fifth house. You are highly original and always are looking for new ways to put forth your ideas. In romantic relationships, you prefer powerful emotional stimuli, and eccentric types appeal to you. Above all, you crave freedom in love and will avoid conventional unions. Your children are independent, high-strung, or rebellious but also very creative and even brilliant.

Neptune in the Fifth House

Artistic, musical, or dramatic talent is evident when Neptune is in the fifth house. You are able to project your imagination through whatever medium you choose. In romantic relationships, you can be too idealistic, unrealistic, or just a willing victim. Your desire to rescue people can attract all sorts of undesirables. Beware of getting caught up in a romantic intrigue. You may sacrifice a lot for your children or to create your dream. You may have psychic talent.

Pluto in the Fifth House

An intense desire to assert your power creatively describes Pluto in the fifth house. Among your talents is the ability to get to the bottom of things, expose the problem, and come up with a solution. Romantic relationships can flourish at times and be absent at others. You want to be in control when in love and may hide your sensitivity from your partner. Children can transform your life in very positive ways.

Planets in the Sixth House

The sixth house describes your work, co-workers, and working environment. It does not indicate career, but rather the work you do to support your career. If you do not have a career, the sixth house shows your job. It defines your capacity for service and voluntary labor. It shows health matters or predisposition to illness, as well as hygiene and nutritional preferences. It further defines domestic pets and small animals.

Sun in the Sixth House

The desire to serve, help others, and be appreciated for your efforts describes the Sun in the sixth house. Your heart must be in what you do in order to sustain your interest. Adept at solving problems, you can light the way for others. Taking good care of your health and all that entails, including nutrition and exercise, is a primary focus. You can be critical or too demanding of yourself because you seek perfection. You work best with others and will create a cheerful working environment.

Moon in the Sixth House

A need to work, provide a service, or care for people describes the Moon in the sixth house. Your workplace is like a second home because you spend so much time there. You can work well with the public or serve the public's needs. Cooking and food preparation can become a vocation. Emotionally sensitive to your working environment, you seek a supportive setting where everyone feels like family. You feel better when you are hard at work taking care of everyone.

Mercury in the Sixth House

Taking care of detailed work defines Mercury in the sixth house. You may wear many hats in your line of work and most likely will move around or travel quite a bit. Communication skills and information gathering are a major part of work activities no matter what career you choose. You can work in pet care, animal rescue, or the health care field. A tendency to worry too much can affect your health, but keeping busy is a good distraction.

Venus in the Sixth House

Pleasant working conditions and favorable employment describe Venus in the sixth house. Your social and diplomatic skills play a role in work activities. The workplace is where your artistic and creative talents come into play. You work well with women and can cater to their needs. You may find employment as a hairstylist, makeup artist, or clothing designer. Your health is usually quite good, though you may have to curb a weakness for sweets.

Mars in the Sixth House

A person who is dynamic, assertive, and energetic, and not one to sit still, describes Mars in the sixth house. You work all the time and prefer to work for yourself. Employees or co-workers cannot keep pace with you; by the time they start, you've completed the task. Your mechanical skills can play a role in your work activities. You may work with computers or other machinery. Your high energy level contributes to good health, though you can benefit from physical activity.

Jupiter in the Sixth House

Good fortune in finding employment and satisfying work defines Jupiter in the sixth house. Wherever you start, you are likely to make progress quickly and end up running the show. Should you work for yourself, you can have success providing a service to others. You are likely to travel in your line of work or at least move around quite a bit. Your co-workers may be from a mix of many different cultures or backgrounds. Your health is generally good, though overindulgence can be an issue.

Saturn in the Sixth House

A strong work ethic and good organizational skills describe Saturn in the sixth house. Your efforts are not immediately acknowledged, but if you persevere, advancement is assured. Capable, conscientious, and efficient, you expect too much of yourself and your co-workers. At some point, you may prefer to be self-employed, making use of your excellent management skills. A tendency to worry or to be too serious affects your health. Learn to laugh a lot.

Uranus in the Sixth House

An unstructured work environment or one in which you can be self-directed define Uranus in the sixth house. Your originality and inventiveness can play a role in your work activities. Working with new technology or high-tech equipment can be part of your job. Sitting at a desk all day is not for you. A highly charged workplace—like the trading floor of the stock exchange—is more appropriate. The more variety and excitement on the job, the better.

Neptune in the Sixth House

Caring for others is often the case when Neptune is in the sixth house. Your sensitivity enables you to be receptive to the needs of those around you. Your artistic talent and imagination can play a role in the work you do. Drawing, animation, photography, or film production are possible vocations. You can work in the music industry or compose music of your own. Sensitivity to your surroundings underlines the importance of a healthy and pleasant workplace.

Pluto in the Sixth House

Passionate about work describes Pluto in the sixth house. With your interest in solving problems, you may be attracted to police or detective work. Courageous and assertive, you may find a career in the armed forces more to your liking. You have the capacity to help people and may consider working in the healing professions; an aptitude for psychology or psychiatry may be evident. Relationships with co-workers can be intense; office politics may be the cause.

Planets in the Seventh House

The seventh house describes your relationships with others, including all those with whom you interact on an equal basis. It shows your marriage partner as well as business partnerships. It also shows the public, including strangers and rivals or those who may become open enemies. Any planet in the seventh house also has an influence on your public persona.

Sun in the Seventh House

Relationships, companionships, and cooperative alliances are a high priority when the Sun is in the seventh house. Your ability to collaborate with others enables you to succeed in partnership ventures. You will attract a spouse or significant other who is confident, devoted, and loyal, though sharing the spotlight will be a necessary component of a happy union. Your self-confidence and creativity are strengthened through the support of your partner.

Moon in the Seventh House

Sensitive and responsive to the needs of others describes the Moon in the seventh house. Your caring nature is extended to all with whom you interact. You can attract a mate who is also quite sensitive and who wants to be nurtured or cared for. Feelings toward partners will fluctuate; restlessness is a dominant theme in your relationships. Business partnerships can experience a continuous cycle of change, but your intuition enables you to stay ahead of the curve.

Mercury in the Seventh House

An analytical and intellectual approach to partnerships describes Mercury in the seventh house. You fall in love with someone's mind before anything else. Your strong desire to communicate and share your thoughts attracts a partner who is witty, inquisitive, and curious. You are likely to form alliances based on common beliefs and ideas. Your public image is one of expertise in your field; you can be an adept and entertaining public speaker.

Venus in the Seventh House

Diplomacy, cooperation, and fairness in alliances describe Venus in the seventh house. Your outgoing way and friendly nature attract many; you will have more than one opportunity for marriage. Your mate is likely to be charming, affectionate, and devoted to you; he or she will improve your financial status. Your public persona can catch the attention of talented, creative people who want to help you. A business partnership can be quite rewarding and profitable.

Mars in the Seventh House

Assertive, confident, and spontaneous in your exchange with others describes Mars in the seventh house. You can attract people who are aggressive and somewhat overbearing. You may act quickly, without thinking things through, when it comes to partnering with another, whether in a business or personal relationship. You are likely to marry early, and your mate will give you a run for your money. In any partnership, you fare better if you can give the other leeway.

Jupiter in the Seventh House

A happy union, marriage, or partnership defines Jupiter in the seventh house. You can marry someone of a different nationality or from a different background than your own. Your mate may introduce you to a world of adventure, travel, and exploration. Partnership ventures can be quite successful and continue to expand and improve over time. Your fondness for marriage, companionship, or cohabitation assures that you will never be single for long.

Saturn in the Seventh House

A cautious approach to relationships defines Saturn in the seventh house. You are likely to remain single until later in life, and in fact this is preferable. An early marriage can be disappointing. You are attracted to someone who is serious, dependable, and steadfast and who will provide you with a sense of security. Business or partnership ventures can be demanding; however, in the long run you can establish a successful enterprise.

Uranus in the Seventh House

An independent temperament keeps you away from the altar when Uranus is in the seventh house. You are likely to remain single unless you find a partner who is flexible and equally self-reliant. Your partnerships exhibit an element of eccentricity, or there is something unusual about the union—you may live apart, for example. You are likely to form alliances with exceptionally talented people who are much younger than you. A business partner can be a genius or an eccentric.

Neptune in the Seventh House

Idealistic, romantic, and impractical about relationships describes Neptune in the seventh house. You can view another through rose-tinted glasses and fail to see any fault. Your sensitivity and compassion draw those who are in need of help, and you may provide counseling. In personal relationships, you will meet two kinds of people: those who are artistic and creative and those who have dependency issues. Make sure you know which type you're dealing with.

Pluto in the Seventh House

Relationships are never trouble-free when Pluto is in the seventh house. You can attract people who are confrontational, emotional, and intense. In business partnerships or alliances, you can run into power struggles, so you may prefer to go it alone. In marriage, you prefer someone who is strong, passionate, and assertive, but never dull. At best, each of you is able to work through unresolved issues and develop a strong bond. Otherwise, the two of you vie for supremacy.

Planets in the Eighth House

The eighth house defines your sexual preferences and interrelationships with others on an intimate level. It shows the manner of your death, not just your physical death but also those experiences that cause you to change and broaden your perspective. This house describes your partner's money and assets; monetary gains from the public; taxes; inheritance; and possessions gained through others.

Sun in the Eighth House

You have the ability to evaluate the resources of others—both material and personal—when the Sun is in the eighth house. You can assist people with their finances, such as in estate or asset management, money lending, or insurance claims. You may work with those who need healing or rehabilitation. Your passionate nature attracts admirers who are equally zealous. Your spouse or business partner can contribute to your financial independence.

Moon in the Eighth House

Sensitive to the needs of others defines the Moon in the eighth house. You may like to nurture or care for those who want help with their problems. Your psychic and intuitive nature is attuned to social currents and trends. You may have a feel for what the public wants and can do well in marketing, promotion, or publicity work. Though you may hide your emotional nature from most people, your feelings surface more easily in intimate relationships.

Mercury in the Eighth House

Good judgment with regard to money and asset management defines Mercury in the eighth house. Creative thinking plays a role in your ability to successfully manage joint resources. Though you are talented and astute in financial areas, you have a tendency to worry about investments. Your powers of observation and analysis enable you to counsel those with problems. Friendship can evolve into an intimate relationship, especially if you share good conversation.

Venus in the Eighth House

Money and assets can be acquired through the marriage partner when Venus is in the eighth house. You also can inherit assets or come into money with little effort. You may have hidden talents such as clairvoyance or other psychic gifts. Receptive to the nonphysical plane, you may be able to act as a medium for others. Passionate and romantic in your intimate relationships, you appreciate someone who will share your love of the good life.

Mars in the Eighth House

Actively engaged in managing the resources of others describes Mars in the eighth house. Your innovative investment strategies can prove successful provided you employ a degree of discipline. Care is needed in handling joint investments and your partner's money to avoid running into debt. Your passionate nature attracts those who are equally fervent, easily roused, or quick-tempered; which it is depends on the aspects to your eighth-house Mars. (Aspects are discussed in the next chapter.)

Jupiter in the Eighth House

Partnership arrangements result in the expansion of assets when Jupiter is in the eighth house. You can benefit financially from your spouse or a business alliance. Investment in foreign markets can prove profitable. You may be able to offer financial advice to others. Borrowing money and acquiring financing are relatively easy. You can take on too much financial risk and overextend yourself. An air of adventure colors your intimate relationships.

Saturn in the Eighth House

Prudent and careful financial planning defines Saturn in the eighth house. You may be good at managing other people's money, though you tend to worry about your own investments. You can teach or instruct others on how to handle their resources. Control of marital assets can be a bone of contention between you and your mate. You have to work hard to find the right balance between spending and saving. Serious about intimate bonds, you are selective in your choice of partners.

Uranus in the Eighth House

Intuition and psychic perception are strong with Uranus in the eighth house. You may have flashes of insight about life after death. You can be creative and innovative in managing partnership assets, though care is needed in forming alliances. A unique approach to asset management may enable you to assist people with tax shelters and investment strategies. Friendship plays an important role in your intimate relationships. Broad-minded about sex, you chafe at social taboos.

Neptune in the Eighth House

Financial returns from an investment or partnership venture can dissipate when Neptune is in the eighth house. Rely on professionals rather than your partners to make financial decisions. Marital assets should be shared and kept fluid to avoid depletion. Your dreams can be very revealing, and you may even have out-of-body experiences. Strongly intuitive and psychic, you may be able to help people develop their unique talents and resources.

Pluto in the Eighth House

Shrewd, tenacious, and resolute, you have the capacity to transform your life when Pluto is in the eighth house. In partnerships and marriage, you prefer to manage all financial decisions; however, you will run up against strong resistance if you're unwilling to share control. You have an innate understanding of life-and-death issues and may be able to assist those who are emotionally or mentally debilitated. Your passionate nature usually is hidden from all but those with whom you share your intimacies.

Planets in the Ninth House

The ninth house describes your advanced education, which could be college, university, seminary, conservatory, academy, or any form of higher learning. It defines your aspirations and religious or spiritual beliefs. This house describes your broadening perspective and the sharing of knowledge; it therefore includes publishing. It shows your extended journeys, especially those that include air travel. Your legal affairs and legal advisors are shown here as well.

Sun in the Ninth House

A student at heart and seeker of knowledge define the Sun in the ninth house. You can develop a broad understanding on many subjects, including philosophy, law, and religion; you may even be interested in pursuing a religious or spiritual path. Foreign cultures, people, and places will likely hold an attraction, and you may travel the world to learn all you can about them. You may marry someone of a foreign background or move a long way from your birth place.

Moon in the Ninth House

Intuitive and receptive to higher consciousness through dreams or visions describe the Moon in the ninth house. You may examine many different religions or spiritual paths in the process of forming your own philosophy of life. Your feelings guide you to a deeper understanding of truth and awareness. You feel comfortable with a variety of cultural influences and may travel or study different traditions. The world is your home.

Mercury in the Ninth House

An interest in opening the mind to higher learning describes Mercury in the ninth house. You analyze and scrutinize different ideologies to get a better understanding of their principles. The legal profession may appeal to you as a means to use your considerable verbal skills. You may have an aptitude for foreign languages and can act as an interpreter or translator. Your versatility in this regard can take you around the world as a foreign correspondent or journalist.

Venus in the Ninth House

Strong attraction or devotion to religious and spiritual ideals defines Venus in the ninth house. You can be dedicated to seeking truth in all forms, and appreciate the similarities among all belief systems. Your love of adventure and faraway places is apt to make you an avid traveler; you may even marry someone from another country. You embrace people of all cultures and value what they have to offer in the way of wisdom. Your charm and grace could make you an ambassador of goodwill.

Mars in the Ninth House

Challenging accepted ideology, ideas, and standards describes Mars in the ninth house. Your enthusiasm, confidence, and assertiveness may find expression in the legal profession, or you may choose the field of education. Whatever your journey, you will seek new ideas and stir things up. Though you can be impatient with others who are slow to change, you never give up the fight. You may travel to far-off places, explore the world through books, or publish your life story.

Jupiter in the Ninth House

Benefits and success through higher education, spiritual studies, writing, and publishing describe Jupiter in the ninth house. Your interest in gathering and disseminating knowledge can give rise to a career in theology, law, or education. An open-minded attitude enables you to embrace many different teachings. Traveling can open doors and offer many opportunities for self-growth. You also may explore the world through books.

Saturn in the Ninth House

A practical approach to learning through experience rather then theorizing defines Saturn in the ninth house. You may have an aptitude for science or any discipline that is methodical, precise, and logical. Your education may take the form of a structured learning environment, such as a private school, academy, or seminary. College or advanced education can be delayed or postponed. A realistic examination of spirituality and religion leads you to form a practical philosophy of your own.

Uranus in the Ninth House

An examination and questioning of existing spiritual, philosophical, and legal knowledge describes Uranus in the ninth house. Whatever principles you were raised with will be challenged. Your intuitive insight guides you to form your own independent conclusions. You may be drawn to a career in broadcasting where you can express your unique brand of wisdom. In your travels, you most likely will visit all those unusual places that are not on the guided tours.

Neptune in the Ninth House

Knowledge gained through a process of introspection rather than external factors defines Neptune in the ninth house. You can be mystical and have psychic perception or spiritual visions. You are able to perceive the common threads among all philosophies and religions. Your attunement to the higher mind may be expressed through extraordinary music or works of art—Henri Matisse had Neptune here. Legal matters can be problematic if you are naïve, gullible, or too trusting.

Pluto in the Ninth House

A discriminating mind and a desire to find the truth behind accepted principles describe Pluto in the ninth house. You have little tolerance for hypocrisy and will form your own conclusions. You love a challenge and may choose the legal profession to make your mark on society. Your strong opinions can influence and persuade others to examine existing laws. You believe in the power of the mind to actualize your dreams and expectations.

Planets in the Tenth House

The tenth house describes your career, profession, or vocation, including your own business. It also shows your reputation, public image, fame or notoriety, and the honors you may receive. It defines the parent of greater influence or the one who takes the dominant role. People who may have authority over you—such as your employer, boss, manager, officials, and judges—also are shown here.

Sun in the Tenth House

A favorable reputation, appropriate use of authority, and focus on career goals describe the Sun in the tenth house. Your leadership abilities enable you to succeed in whatever career you choose. You can garner favorable attention and gain the support of your peers. Not one to sit on the sidelines, you like the spotlight and the prestige that goes along with success. Your many talents are expressed in your profession, and you most likely will attain status and recognition.

Moon in the Tenth House

You are likely to travel many different paths before finding the right profession with the Moon in the tenth house. Your sensitivity to what the public wants can bring success in catering to their needs. The food, restaurant, or hotel business can be good career choices. Anything to do with building, land development, or home design may offer other opportunities. Though you are comfortable remaining behind the scenes, your image or work may appear in the public arena.

Mercury in the Tenth House

An interest in communicating thoughts and ideas through your chosen profession describes Mercury in the tenth house. Your keen observation and ability to convey what you see can lead to a career in journalism, broadcasting, writing, or reporting. You can be an educator or counselor. The transportation industry or travel business are viable alternatives when Mercury is in the tenth house. One of your parents is an intellect with a lively sense of humor.

Venus in the Tenth House

The power of attraction and personal charm contributes to career success when Venus is in the tenth house. Your artistic and creative talent is expressed through your profession. Some examples of vocational choices include curator of an art gallery or a position in the beauty industry or in fashion or jewelry design. Your social skills and friendly manner can assist you with a career in public relations. You're recognized for your style and good taste. One of your parents may be in the arts.

Mars in the Tenth House

Initiative, action, and energy are directed toward the achievement of career goals when Mars is in the tenth house. Your take-charge attitude can put you in a leadership position. You prefer to be your own boss, assuming a hands-on approach to your work. Some possible choices include machinist, mechanic, competitive athlete, engineer, or a career in the military. You like to be challenged in whatever you do, and your ambitious, competitive nature helps you succeed.

Jupiter in the Tenth House

Career success and a fine reputation often are endowed when Jupiter is in the tenth house. Your generous nature and fair dealings with people attract those who are supportive and help you succeed. You want to achieve something meaningful and improve circumstances for others. The field of education, medicine, theology, foreign affairs, or high finance are possible career choices with Jupiter in the tenth house. You can be honored for your professional accomplishments.

Saturn in the Tenth House

Self-reliance and perseverance help you achieve career goals when Saturn is in the tenth house. Your work ethic, organizational abilities, and good judgment favor success in business. Integrity grants you power to accomplish whatever you will; the lack of it threatens a fall from grace. Other than business, a career in science, medical research, archeology, building, or construction may be of interest. Your patience and determination enable you to reach the pinnacle of your profession.

Uranus in the Tenth House

Creativity, originality, and individuality preclude an ordinary profession when Uranus is in the tenth house. You are not one to conform to rigid standards and almost always strike out on your own. Humanitarian interests can take you on a different career path than you had planned. A career in computer science, electronics, technology, aviation, television broadcasting, or astrology are some possibilities. You can set forth new ideas or invent something wonderful.

Neptune in the Tenth House

Artistic talent and creative imagination can be expressed through your career when Neptune is in the tenth house. You may have an aptitude for the dramatic arts; many film stars have Neptune here. This planet gives the ability to project an image and create an illusion. You also can have success with a musical career. More often, your compassion and concern for others finds expression in the medical profession or social services. You can work in an institutional setting such as a nursing home or hospital.

Pluto in the Tenth House

Ingenuity, cunning, and determination help you achieve career goals when Pluto is in the tenth house. Your capacity to transform and heal could lead to a career in the medical field. Your professional objectives often are connected with helping others manage their resources, both material and spiritual. Other possible career choices include psychiatry and psychology, asset management, police and detective work, demolition, and volcanology. You almost always work for yourself.

Planets in the Eleventh House

The eleventh house describes your acquaintances, friends, companions, and casual relationships. It defines your hopes, wishes, aspirations, and ideals. This is where your dreams are realized. It shows your group affiliations, club memberships, and humanitarian interests and endeavors. Income earned from business and the resources of the business are shown here.

Sun in the Eleventh House

Friendships play a part in the realization of goals when the Sun is in the eleventh house. Your friends are influential people who support your endeavors. As a group member, you can shine a spotlight on circumstances that need changing and bring your power to bear on needed reform. Your strength inspires others to stand up and make a difference. Your talent, creativity, and positive attitude enable you to achieve what you wish for.

Moon in the Eleventh House

Goals and aspirations undergo many different phases when the Moon is in the eleventh house. You can embrace diverse paths before arriving at your true calling. Sensitive and receptive, you are supportive of your friends and responsive to their needs. Your friendships often take the place of family, and provide a support system in your life. The care and nurturing goes both ways; sometimes you take a parental role and other times you're on the receiving end.

Mercury in the Eleventh House

The wish to communicate thoughts and ideas is a strong objective when Mercury is in the eleventh house. You may want to write about new insights and share your creative ideas with others. Your communication skills play a part in advancing what you aspire to accomplish. Though your aspirations may change as you analyze and reassess what is meaningful, you will never give up the quest for enlightenment. Friendships are based on good communication and a meeting of the minds.

Venus in the Eleventh House

Social contacts and friendships are influential in the attainment of goals when Venus is in the eleventh house. You can meet people who want to help you advance your interests. Your values and principles are admired by many, and you can bring others together for a common cause. You are blessed with lots of friends whose only wish is to help you attain your dreams. You love people and will get involved whenever you can contribute something to the group.

Mars in the Eleventh House

Assertive action to achieve goals and objectives describes Mars in the eleventh house. The phrase "Be careful what you wish for" is one to ponder; you can rush into things without pausing to consider the consequences. Your optimism and enthusiasm can be focused on improving conditions for many. Friends are likely to share your passions, though competitiveness can get in the way of friendship. You may have sports in common or similar lifestyles.

Jupiter in the Eleventh House

Idealistic and adventurous in the pursuit of wishes describes Jupiter in the eleventh house. You can explore many different paths on the way to attaining your objectives. You may have friends from various backgrounds and cultures who stimulate diverse interests. Friends offer benefits, open doors, and can help you accomplish what you want. You are likely to enjoy the company of people who are wise and gifted and who encourage you to reach for your dreams.

Saturn in the Eleventh House

The attainment of goals and ambitions is delayed but not denied when Saturn is in the eleventh house. Your perseverance will be rewarded, and your dreams, once realized, are lasting. Your accomplishments increase with age, as do your rewards, as long as you continue to work toward that end. Your friends may be fewer in number, though you have many acquaintances. You enjoy spending time with the select circle of friends you have cultivated over time.

Uranus in the Eleventh House

An unexpected change in life direction describes Uranus in the eleventh house. Your hopes and dreams take on a life of their own, and you end up where you least expected. This is good news, because your wishes have a way of materializing. Blessed with insight and intuition, you can find the best way to accomplish something. Your creative thinking can change circumstances, and everyone benefits. Your friends run the gamut from eccentric and creative to peculiar and strange.

Neptune in the Eleventh House

Aspirations and objectives have to be defined and unambiguous when Neptune is in the eleventh house. Your sensitivity and creativity can play a positive role in the pursuit of your goals. You can be too idealistic in what you wish for, but your dreams have a way of materializing when you least expect it. Your friends may vary from artistic and creative to needy and codependent. You are more likely to foster constructive friendships among those who are spiritual, gifted, or talented.

Pluto in the Eleventh House

A determined and unwavering pursuit of personal goals and ambitions describes Pluto in the eleventh house. Your ingenuity can result in success, but take care to define what you really want, for you will get it. You have a knack for eliminating wasteful spending and creating an atmosphere of renewal. Your friendships are likely to go through a transitional phase, but those who remain are loyal to the end. You value friends who share your desire to unravel life's mysteries.

Planets in the Twelfth House

The twelfth house describes areas of seclusion and places of confinement, like prisons, institutions, hospitals, and monasteries. It also shows constructive withdrawal to participate in that which is creative or enlightening, such as writing, composing music, or engaging in spiritual practices. This house further defines where you can deceive yourself; it therefore is called the house of self-undoing. It shows hidden matters and charitable deeds.

Sun in the Twelfth House

A strong desire to be of help to others and to work behind the scenes describes the Sun in the twelfth house. You have a compassionate nature and can care for those who are afflicted. Research, writing, composing, and other such solitary vocations may appeal to you. Your need for serenity can cause you to withdraw from the clamor of everyday life to seek privacy. You may enjoy a spiritual retreat or simply some alone time in your favorite setting.

Moon in the Twelfth House

Psychic and receptive to the feelings of others defines the Moon in the twelfth house. A very sensitive nature aids in your ability to nurture those who need assistance. You can feel overwhelmed at times and may try to hide your emotions rather than appear vulnerable. Your instincts are valid and can assist you in developing higher spiritual awareness. You have empathy for those who are ailing, needy, or disadvantaged and may feel the need to help better their lives.

Mercury in the Twelfth House

Thoughts and ideas focused on solitary endeavors like writing or research define Mercury in the twelfth house. You may provide counsel or other services to those with intellectual or physical disabilities. Interested in expanding your consciousness, you may practice meditation or pursue other spiritual endeavors. Your communication skills can raise awareness for charitable events. Comfortable with the knowledge that there are many paths to awareness, you're content to keep your thoughts to yourself.

Venus in the Twelfth House

A compassionate nature often focused on an ideal describes Venus in the twelfth house. You desire to give assistance—in one form or another— to those who need help. The knowledge that someone may benefit from what you have to offer gives you joy. Your happiness rarely comes from worldly matters but is tied to the nonmaterial or spiritual aspects of life. Emotional and secretive about your feelings, you love spending time by yourself. You feel a strong connection to all things.

Mars in the Twelfth House

Your drive for power usually is directed inward when Mars is in the twelfth house. You may actively pursue studies of occult subjects, mysticism, or spirituality. Initiative and assertiveness—qualities you possess—can be used to influence others and organize support for your favorite charity. Though you may appear passive, you are a formidable opponent when your principles are challenged. You can expend a great deal of energy working behind the scenes for the benefit of the greater good.

Jupiter in the Twelfth House

A broad understanding of many of life's deeper mysteries describes Jupiter in the twelfth house. You're interested in growth and expansion of the spiritual kind and may explore different beliefs or choose to live a religious life. You can inspire others to live a better life through your example; the inner joy you radiate is apparent to everyone. If interested in teaching, you may prefer an institutional setting, such as a hospital. Benefits are bestowed when you least expect it.

Saturn in the Twelfth House

A conscientious endeavor to serve the needs of others describes Saturn in the twelfth house. Though at times you may want to retreat from the world, when duty calls you always come through. Your organizational skills help you accomplish a great deal from behind the scenes, and you elicit everyone's best effort. Determined to understand life's deeper meaning, you work to uncover spiritual truths. Your perseverance is rewarded with wisdom born of experience.

Uranus in the Twelfth House

Inventiveness and creativity directed toward the needs of the many define Uranus in the twelfth house. You can focus your imagination and vision on scientific research, new technologies, or a favorite cause. Your early experiences may have caused you to hide your eccentricities, but once revealed, the possibilities are endless—a new invention, for instance. Your love of freedom may keep you from making commitments until you remember that you already are free.

Neptune in the Twelfth House

Sensitivity and compassion toward those who are suffering describe Neptune in the twelfth house. Your attunement to the higher self gives solace and enables you to guide others on the spiritual path. A gentle nature and willingness to help people may draw you to work in the medical profession. You can spend many a joyful hour in the quiet solitude of your own mind. Periodic withdrawal from the clamor of everyday life helps renew your soul.

Pluto in the Twelfth House

Power directed toward the transformation of others defines Pluto in the twelfth house. You can heal—physically, emotionally, or psychologically—those who need healing. Psychiatry, psychology, and the mental health field may appeal to you. Deeply philosophical, you can pursue a spiritual discipline with great zeal. Your strong psychic connection with "all that is" gives you access to knowing that cannot be put into words. Though you are an emotional being, you may hide your intense feelings.

PLANETS IN THE SIGNS

Planets in Aries ♈

Any planet in Aries will take on the active, dynamic, outgoing characteristics of this cardinal fire sign. Among the qualities associated with Aries are a competitive nature, confidence, initiative, and a desire for adventure.

Sun in Aries

The Sun in Aries person likes to be first at everything. You are confident, energetic, and enthusiastic about life. You are always in a hurry to move on to the next adventure, and your impatience can get in the way of smooth relationships. You're eager to try your hand at something new as long as it offers a challenge. You courageously take the lead in most situations and rarely like taking directions from others.

Moon in Aries

The Moon in Aries person is impetuous. Your feelings are more easily hurt than one would think because you give the impression that you are invincible. On the contrary, you are emotionally sensitive, spontaneous, and quick to respond to others. Your courage is admirable, but you may hide some insecurity. You feel things with intensity and can be impulsive, but you are a loyal and enthusiastic person.

Mercury in Aries

The Mercury in Aries person is attentive. You like a challenge and always look for new ways to express your ideas. You are a true believer in the power of positive thinking, and your enthusiasm is catching. Articulate, dynamic, and direct, you have a way of stimulating interest and stirring things up; you could be a powerful motivational speaker. Your strength lies in your ability to come up with new ideas and think outside the box.

Venus in Aries

The Venus in Aries person is ardent. You love with passion and enthusiasm but may find it hard to sustain that feeling after a while. You are impulsive and idealistic, and your feelings are easily hurt, though you never let on. You enjoy the chase and crave excitement in your relationships. By keeping it fresh, you can avoid the risk of becoming bored. Your energy and intensity are very appealing, and you always attract new admirers.

Mars in Aries

The Mars in Aries person is assertive. Your high energy level and need to be busy keep you on the go and very likely slim and fit. Courageous and confident, you can take positive action more quickly than most people. Your independent nature is attractive to those who are equally strong. You can be impulsive—charging right in—and may have to work on follow-through. Inner restlessness is hard to quell.

Jupiter in Aries

The Jupiter in Aries person is enthusiastic. You are the eternal optimist whose strong self-esteem attracts many opportunities. Your confidence and originality enable you to strike out in new directions. Strong leadership and executive abilities help you to do well in business or any area of interest. When you take the initiative, new ventures can pay off in a big way. Travel can open doors and bring more success.

Saturn in Aries

The Saturn in Aries person is a leader. Your logic and reasoning are solid, though you may have less confidence in yourself than others have in you. You can take the initiative and argue your point successfully. Self-employment is preferable because you may have conflicts with those in authority. Your energy may be sluggish, but you can benefit from keeping yourself physically active.

Uranus in Aries

The Uranus in Aries person is inquisitive. You have an ingenious ability to come up with new and creative ideas that improve conditions for everyone. Your pioneering spirit and energetic approach can attract attention and help you succeed. Because you are confident in your vision, it is easy for you to get others on board with your plans. Your unique insights enable you to bring new concepts into focus.

Neptune in Aries

The Neptune in Aries person is inspirational. Because Neptune remains in a sign for fourteen years, it will influence an entire generation. It was last in Aries in the mid-1800s. At that time, there was great interest in the new spirituality called Theosophy. Neptune will not be in Aries again until 2026. Perhaps it will foster another spiritual awakening.

Pluto in Aries

Pluto moves slowly and has an irregular orbit, remaining in a sign for anywhere from twelve to twenty-two years. Since Pluto was not discovered until 1930, we have not observed it in Aries since its discovery. Pluto will move into Aries in 2068. Because Pluto remains in a sign for an extended period, it influences an entire generation. We can only speculate that Pluto in Aries may give rise to a new generation of explorers.

Planets in Taurus ♉

Any planet in Taurus will exhibit the patience, practicality, and reliability associated with this fixed earth sign. Among the qualities expressed with Taurus are loyalty, persistence, tenacity, dependability, and affection.

Sun in Taurus

With the Sun in Taurus, you may take a while to get going, but you will persevere until the job is done. Not one to be foolhardy, you think things through before making decisions, and once your mind is made up, you are unlikely to change it. Your dedication, strong work ethic, and practical financial decisions can lead to success in business. Change is difficult for you, and you are likely to mull things over for a long while before altering course.

Moon in Taurus

The Moon in Taurus person is generous. You love all the good things life can offer, including financial security, rich foods, and a beautiful home. Your emotional steadiness enables you to stay focused even in difficult situations. Good-natured and resourceful, you feel comfortable among those who share your conservative values. The accumulation of material assets is quite important, though you are willing to share what you have.

Mercury in Taurus

The Mercury in Taurus person is disciplined. You put a great deal of thought into achieving financial independence and establishing a solid foundation. Cautious and deliberate, you make decisions that are geared toward long-term security for yourself and your loved ones. Creative thinking and an artistic flair can contribute to success in business. You trust your judgment and cannot be easily influenced by another's opinion.

Venus in Taurus

The Venus in Taurus person is loyal. Your affectionate nature and sensuality can be quite attractive to the opposite sex. Emotional and loving, you are truly happy only when you have someone with whom to share your life. Material comforts are important, and you appreciate stylish, elegant, and beautiful things. Artistic and talented, you can excel in any field in which creativity is desired. Dessert is the way to your heart.

Mars in Taurus

The Mars in Taurus person is unrelenting. Your persistence and patience far exceed the norm, and eventually you get what you want. A strong work ethic aids in the accumulation of material assets and substance. Practical and sensible about money matters, you make wise financial decisions. You can be possessive of those you love, but your loyalty is not in question. Once you decide to go after something, there's no stopping you.

Jupiter in Taurus

The Jupiter in Taurus person is magnanimous. You have an abundance of artistic and creative talent, which can be expressed in any number of ways. Your financial acumen enables you to generate money, accumulate assets, and make sound investments. You love luxurious things and take pride in owning collectibles. Foreign investment can prove to be financially rewarding. Generous with money and resources, you like to share what you have with others.

Saturn in Taurus

The Saturn in Taurus person is dedicated. Your determination and unwavering commitment to any project ensure success. You may be overly concerned with material security but worry needlessly. Establishing financial freedom requires a combination of persistence and diligence—qualities you possess in abundance. The more willing you are to share responsibility and to delegate some authority, the bigger and better your accomplishments.

Uranus in Taurus

The Uranus in Taurus person is productive. Your insights with regard to financial matters can be ingenious or radical. Flashes of inspiration may guide you toward new and creative business opportunities. Your relationships can be somewhat unpredictable or unconventional, especially if Uranus is in aspect with Venus (see the next chapter). However, there is also the potential for new adventures, excitement, and happiness in your partnerships.

Neptune in Taurus

The Neptune in Taurus person is talented. Because Neptune remains in a sign for fourteen years, it will influence an entire generation. It was last in Taurus in the late 1800s and will not be in this sign again until 2038. We can only speculate that Neptune in Taurus may give rise to a generation that covets material wealth or one that relinquishes it.

Pluto in Taurus

Pluto moves slowly and has an irregular orbit, remaining in a sign for anywhere from twelve to twenty-two years. Since Pluto was not discovered until 1930, we have not observed it in Taurus since its discovery. Pluto will not move into Taurus until the next century. Because Pluto remains in a sign for an extended period, it influences an entire generation. We can only speculate that Pluto in Taurus may give rise to a generation that challenges the values of the times.

Planets in Gemini ♊

Any planet in Gemini will display strong communicative tendencies, adaptability, and curiosity. Among the other qualities associated with this mutable air sign are inventiveness, tolerance, and an affinity for analysis.

Sun in Gemini

Your interests are so diversified that you generally have several irons in the fire and may have difficulty focusing on one thing at a time. Constant communications keep you informed on many topics and in touch with everyone in your life. Sometimes worrisome and restless, you prefer to keep going even when you have no particular destination. You are one of those people who can do several things at once.

Moon in Gemini

The Moon in Gemini person is restless. You're easily bored and need to keep busy to feel good. You're curious about many things, and your search for knowledge is a lifelong mission. Your memory for trivia can be quite amazing, and you enjoy learning something about every subject of interest. You prefer to browse through many topics rather than undertake an in-depth study. Discussing your feelings is important for emotional release.

Mercury in Gemini

The Mercury in Gemini person is multitalented. You may be described as a good conversationalist, witty, and entertaining. Sometimes you can jump to the wrong conclusion, especially when you are tired or stressed. Your mind is so active that you may feel overwhelmed with too much information. Try listening to your feelings, which may require practice because you tend to overanalyze things.

Venus in Gemini

The Venus in Gemini person is fickle. Charming and entertaining, you make friends and form relationships easily. Though you are loving and caring, it may be hard for you to commit to one person when there are so many to choose from. You enjoy your freedom and may prefer to play the field. When you do fall in love, it will be with someone with whom you can talk and share your ideas on all levels.

Mars in Gemini

The Mars in Gemini person is adaptable. Afraid to miss anything, you can take on too many projects and spread yourself thin. Your versatility enables you to do many things well, though you need focus and discipline. Quick to take action, you have good mechanical skills. When you concentrate your power, you can accomplish more in one day than most people do in ten. You may be somewhat critical of those who are not as capable as you.

Jupiter in Gemini

The Jupiter in Gemini person is ingenious. You may express your many creative ideas in writing. Likely to have an aptitude for words and dialects, you may be fluent in several different languages. Your love of books can lead to a career in publishing. You may do well in the travel business, sales, or teaching. You are interested in learning all you can and in expanding your understanding on every level.

Saturn in Gemini

The Saturn in Gemini person is studious. You are knowledgeable about many things and good at teaching or instructing others. Your ability to focus intently on any subject of interest would make you a good analyst, researcher, investigator, or explorer. You are willing to listen to many points of view as long as you are free to communicate your own ideas.

Uranus in Gemini

The Uranus in Gemini person is original. Your ability to grasp new concepts and express innovative ideas is likely to attract attention. You are not afraid to challenge accepted principles or to question the powers that be. A good education is an important consideration, and you are likely to acquire knowledge on many subjects. You may have an aptitude for writing or other fields of communication like television broadcasting or journalism.

Neptune in Gemini

The Neptune in Gemini person is poetic. Because Neptune remains in a sign for fourteen years, it will influence an entire generation. It was last in Gemini in the late 1800s, during which time advances in commerce were made. Neptune will not be in Gemini again until 2052. We can only speculate that Neptune in Gemini may give rise to a socially conscious generation.

Pluto in Gemini

Pluto moves slowly and has an irregular orbit, remaining in a sign for anywhere from twelve to twenty-two years. Since Pluto was not discovered until 1930, we have not observed it in Gemini since its discovery. Pluto will not move into Gemini until the next century. Because Pluto remains in a sign for an extended period, it influences an entire generation. We can only speculate that Pluto in Gemini may give rise to a generation willing to challenge the ideas of the times.

Planets in Cancer ♋

Any planet in Cancer will express the sensitivity and nurturing instincts of this cardinal water sign. Cancer is receptive, maternal, imaginative, intuitive, emotional, and domestic. There will be a clear tendency to protect and shelter.

Sun in Cancer

The Sun in Cancer person is nurturing. Your caring and emotional nature can cause you to be too sensitive to everyone's needs at the expense of your own. You don't mind catering to others as long as your efforts are appreciated. Keen intuition guides your decisions; you can easily sense others' moods. When you're around happy people, you're likely to flourish, whereas the opposite is true when exposed to gloomy types.

Moon in Cancer

The Moon in Cancer person is responsive. You are happiest when you can nurture and care for someone who in turn provides you with a sense of security. Emotional sensitivity is so acute that you can feel overwhelmed at times, but keeping active and busy is a good antidote. Your dedication to family has its rewards in the pride you take in their accomplishments. A keen memory helps you retain every experience, and you never forget an emotional hurt.

Mercury in Cancer

The Mercury in Cancer person is intuitive. Your uncanny ability to reflect whatever you observe is a double-edged sword. On the one hand, your sensitivity can cause you to be indecisive; on the other, your ability to mirror social conditions can garner a measure of success or even fame. Emotional impressions are uppermost in your mind when making decisions; you follow your instincts most of the time.

Venus in Cancer

The Venus in Cancer person is sentimental. Affectionate and kind, you love to be cared for and in turn give emotional support to all those around you. You are happiest when you feel secure and will search for that special someone who offers stability. Your nurturing instincts may surface in romantic relationships, though you can attract someone who wants to look after you. There is a softness and vulnerability about you that others find appealing.

Mars in Cancer

The Mars in Cancer person is expressive. If someone wants to motivate you, he or she has to appeal to your emotions. You rarely take action without feeling inspired. Likewise, you are good at arousing others and may be an excellent team leader or coach. You can channel your emotional energy through something creative, like cooking, or something more physical, like sports. Quite a few chefs have Mars in Cancer, as do many athletes.

Jupiter in Cancer

The Jupiter in Cancer person is kindhearted. Your gregarious personality may serve you well in the public arena; people are attracted to your openness. You're generous with what you have and are sensitive to the needs of others. You can be lucky with real estate and land development. Your intuition plays an important part in your ability to accumulate funds; follow your instincts. You can have substantial assets at an early age.

Saturn in Cancer

The Saturn in Cancer person is shy. A tendency to guard your feelings hides a soft, sensitive side that others rarely see. You are insightful and even cunning when it comes to assessing what motivates people, and you can use this trait to your advantage. As long as you feel safe and secure, there's no limit to what you can accomplish; thus, a stable home is important. Serious on the outside, you can be quite the comedian once you let down your guard.

Uranus in Cancer

The Uranus in Cancer person is instinctive. Your emotional nature may seem detached, because your main goal is to be free from attachment. You may be unconventional in your approach to raising a family, or have an unusual relationship with your mother. Your ability to understand emotional complexities can help you in counseling others. You may have unique insight into the subconscious mind.

Neptune in Cancer

The Neptune in Cancer person is overly sensitive. Because Neptune remains in a sign for fourteen years, it will influence an entire generation. It was last in Cancer during World War I, a time when many families sacrificed loved ones. Neptune will not move into Cancer again until late in the twenty-first century. We can only speculate that its next foray into Cancer may foster a generation that values family above all else.

Pluto in Cancer

The Pluto in Cancer person is resilient. Those born from 1914 to 1939 have this placement. This is the generation that experienced the Great Depression and endured many hardships. Those born during this cycle are concerned mainly with family values, home, and country. Many went to war to protect their homeland. With this placement, you will fight to protect all that is near and dear to your heart.

Planets in Leo ♌

Any planet in Leo will operate in a dramatic and confident way. Among the qualities associated with this fixed fire sign are loyalty, dignity, and strength. Generosity and a gregarious nature will be evident.

Sun in Leo

The Sun in Leo person is proud. Your confidence and assurance motivate others, especially when you assume a leadership role. Playful and fun-loving, you can get along well with children because you have never lost your childlike wonder. Highly creative and fond of the spotlight, you may be attracted to the public arena. Your talents can be displayed on stage and/or before an audience. Many theatrical people have the Sun in Leo.

Moon in Leo

The Moon in Leo person is showy. You love when people fuss over you, but you're just as happy when you can do the same for someone else. Proud of your heritage, you display an air of authority, and people tend to think of you as a leader. Though you can be offended if denied respect, you may hide this tendency from others. Your warmth, affectionate nature, and sociability draw plenty of attention from the opposite sex.

Mercury in Leo

The Mercury in Leo person is dramatic. You convey your thoughts and ideas with heart, and people find you likable and engaging. Your refined way of speaking is entertaining, and you don't mind being asked to give your opinion on any subject. With a genuine desire to empower people, you can motivate those with whom you come in contact. You easily see the big picture, though you prefer to let someone else handle the details.

Venus in Leo

The Venus in Leo person is ardent. Your compassion and kindness toward others are recognized by all who know you. Loyal and affectionate, you are honest in your relationships and love to share good times with those you care about. Nothing but the best appeals to you, whether it is clothing, an automobile, or a vacation. You want to enjoy the optimum experience at every level. Sincere and resolute, you cannot be persuaded unless it's your choice.

Mars in Leo

The Mars in Leo person is fearless. You pursue your goals with enthusiasm and rarely let obstacles get in the way. Your passion for life is evident, and coupled with high energy, you are a force to behold. Dramatic and courageous, you can attract attention to promote your objectives. You take an active role in the lives of those you love, though you can be a little overzealous. Your vitality keeps you physically active and youthful throughout your life.

Jupiter in Leo

The Jupiter in Leo person is vibrant. You like doing things in a big way and may be somewhat extravagant, but you certainly know how to draw attention to your projects. Your self-reliance impresses the right people, and you can assume an executive role. You take pride in your accomplishments and want to be noticed for what you have done. Though you may go out of your way to impress people, your heart is in the right place.

Saturn in Leo

The Saturn in Leo person is admirable. You show great strength and dignity in the pursuit of your objectives, and value the respect you earn from your colleagues. You take pride in your creative endeavors and can be quite successful in the arts. Your leadership qualities and mental clarity enable you to stay a step ahead of the competition; you ultimately garner rewards or recognition for your efforts.

Uranus in Leo

The Uranus in Leo person is original. Determined to break down barriers, you can be innovative in your chosen field. Unique insight into the power structure enables you to expose inequities and introduce new concepts for all to consider. Your strong convictions and insightful assessment of social needs can help you make changes for the better. With vitality and determination, you stir things up and find new ways to get the job done.

Neptune in Leo

The Neptune in Leo person is lenient. Because Neptune remains in a sign for fourteen years, it will influence an entire generation. It was last in Leo from 1915 to 1929, during the Roaring Twenties, when people were obsessed with living life to the fullest. It will not move into Leo again until the late twenty-first century. We can only speculate that it may foster a generation of very creative individuals.

Pluto in Leo

The Pluto in Leo person is individualistic and idealistic. This is the generation born between 1939 and 1958. Those born during this generation included the baby boomers, who challenged authority at every level. They were determined to bring about changes, and so they have.

Planets in Virgo ♍

Any planet in Virgo will exhibit strong analytical and detail-oriented tendencies. Among the qualities associated with this mutable earth sign are honesty, efficiency, and dependability. Organizational skills, discrimination, and precision will be evident.

Sun in Virgo

The Sun in Virgo person is humane. Your desire for perfection—both in yourself and in others—is at the heart of your unending attention to detail. You are always helpful and willing to serve and prefer to work quietly behind the scenes. Your inquisitive nature and powers of discrimination enable you to analyze and solve problems that others miss. Satisfaction comes from working with people and using your many skills productively.

Moon in Virgo

The Moon is Virgo person is particular. Self-critical, you never think your efforts are good enough, but a genuine desire to help people can allay your anxiety. In fact, you are happiest when you keep busy to dispel feelings of insecurity. Honest, dependable, versatile, and skilled, you work well in many arenas. You tend to worry endlessly about little things, but your caring nature is evident to everyone.

Mercury in Virgo

The Mercury in Virgo person is analytical. Your penchant for detail and strong communication skills enable you to be a convincing speaker and good debater. Common sense and a practical mindset assist in bringing others around to your point of view. You may assume that logic will prevail in all matters and have a low tolerance for those who cannot listen to reason. Your intelligence and sincerity are admired by your peers.

Venus in Virgo

The Venus in Virgo person is selective. Your tendency to look for the perfect partner may keep you from a potentially satisfying experience, so take a chance once in a while. You may have a talent for intricate design or detailed work such as architectural drawings. Your desire to help people is a dominant theme in your life, and much of your time is devoted to work. It's possible to meet a love interest through your work or in the work setting.

Mars in Virgo

The Mars in Virgo person is fastidious. You are an energetic worker and give full attention to detail no matter what the objective. Your kindness and interest in helping others play an important part in the work you choose. Practical and ingenious, you can cut to the chase and find the best way to do something. You're willing to go all out and give your best but have little tolerance for those who won't.

Jupiter in Virgo

The Jupiter in Virgo person is humanitarian. Your interest in helping people develop their skills makes you a good teacher, counselor, or coach. You have the ability to gather detailed information and may have an interest in research and investigative work. An aptitude for analytical analysis can give you the edge in journalism, broadcasting, or political commentary. You can be overwhelmed with details, so try to compartmentalize your projects.

Saturn in Virgo

The Saturn in Virgo person is a perfectionist. You like to keep busy, so work is more than just a way to make a living—it's part of your nature. Your discipline and efficiency enable you to do detailed research or scientific study. You strive for excellence and do not hesitate to accept responsibilities but may have a tendency to worry needlessly. Serious and diligent, you find it hard to relax and just do nothing at all.

Uranus in Virgo

The Uranus in Virgo person is compassionate. Your ability to implement new and innovative ways of doing things can gain you a reputation as a creative thinker. You may contribute to advances in alternative health care or natural health products. You can offer ways to improve the workplace or create a better working environment. Your genius lies in your ability to propagate new ideas, raise awareness, and stimulate people to get involved.

Neptune in Virgo

The Neptune in Virgo person is thoughtful. Since Neptune remains in a sign for fourteen years, it influences an entire generation. It was last in Virgo from 1929 to 1943, during the time of the Great Depression. This is the generation that made great sacrifices just to survive. If you were born with Neptune in Virgo, you are compassionate and willing to help others. Neptune will not be in Virgo again until the next century.

Pluto in Virgo

Pluto moves slowly and has an irregular orbit, remaining in a sign for anywhere from twelve to twenty-two years. It therefore influences an entire generation. Pluto was last in Virgo from 1956 to 1971 and will not be there again until the next century. If you were born with Pluto in Virgo, you may contribute to reforming the health care system. Your interest in natural foods, healthy living, and a clean environment can bring about changes in these areas.

Planets in Libra ♎

Any planet in Libra will display a balanced approach to everything. Among the qualities associated with this cardinal air sign are diplomacy, consideration, and a friendly, sociable attitude. Flexibility and a sense of fairness will be evident.

Sun in Libra

The Sun in Libra person is sociable. Your diplomatic skills are known to many, but what is less well known is your ability to counter every argument with opposing facts. You are a good debater and ultimately succeed in presenting a balanced picture. You can be aggressive and passive all at once and manage to charm everyone in the process. Interested in unity, you can act as an intermediary or mediator.

Moon in Libra

The Moon in Libra person is outgoing. Gentle in nature, you dislike friction and create a welcoming home that reflects your grace and style. Ambitious but amiable, you can achieve your goals more easily with a supportive partner to provide emotional balance. You very much want to be liked by everyone and may be hesitant to take sides if it means alienating someone. Your strength often is masked by charisma that is disarming.

Mercury in Libra

The Mercury in Libra person is agreeable. It may take you a while to make up your mind because you weigh everything so carefully. Your good judgment and positive attitude help you see both sides of an issue. You are high-minded and principled, and it can be difficult for others to live up to your standards. But your powers of persuasion and charming personality win everyone over to your point of view.

Venus in Libra

The Venus in Libra person is romantic. Your social graces and easy rapport with people make you the perfect host. You are artistic and creative, and your surroundings reflect a love of beautiful things, a sense of color, and good taste. A good conversationalist, you like to interact with others who are refined and sophisticated. Though you are sensitive and easily hurt, you may be somewhat impersonal in your relationships.

Mars in Libra

The Mars in Libra person is fair. You are a keen observer, and nothing motivates you like injustice. Though you can see both sides of an argument, you will fight to protect freedom of choice. Generally easygoing, you can be quite the warrior if cornered. You may prefer diplomacy to ultimatums but can switch strategies at will. Relationships can be problematic until the balance between self-interest and self-sacrifice is achieved.

Jupiter in Libra

The Jupiter in Libra person is gregarious. Your ability to relate to people, coupled with a friendly, outgoing nature, attracts opportunity through partnerships, both business and personal. Broad-minded and impartial in your dealings with others, you may be successful working in the public sector or in your own business. You prefer to do things in concert with others.

Saturn in Libra

The Saturn in Libra person is devoted. Your commitment to fair play and willingness to meet the other person halfway help you form successful alliances. When you enter into a personal relationship, you are dedicated to its success. Sensing your wisdom, others may turn to you for sage advice, especially when it comes to matters of the heart. Marriage may be delayed, but it endures once you decide to embrace it.

Uranus in Libra

The Uranus in Libra person is distinctive. Your individuality and commitment to freedom lead to an unconventional approach to marriage and relationships in general. Insightful when it comes to legal issues, you can help break down barriers and reform legislation. Your artistic and creative expression is unique, leaning toward exciting colors, unusual decor, and different kinds of music.

Neptune in Libra

The Neptune in Libra person is an idealist. Since Neptune remains in a sign for fourteen years, it influences an entire generation. It was last in Libra from 1943 to 1957, during the time when people were recovering from World War II. This generation grew up in 1960s espousing the virtues of love and peace. If you were born with Neptune in Libra, you idealize those you love, and sacrifice to maintain harmony in your relationships.

Pluto in Libra

Pluto moves slowly and has an irregular orbit, remaining in a sign for anywhere from twelve to twenty-two years. It therefore influences an entire generation. Pluto was last in Libra from 1972 to 1984 and will not be there again until the next century. If you were born with Pluto in Libra, you may be influential in helping to reform our legal system. Your generation's ideas about marriage may be revolutionary and lead to change in legislation.

Planets in Scorpio ♏

Any planet in Scorpio will exhibit tenacity and intensity, though actions may not be out in the open. Among the qualities associated with this fixed water sign are courage, assertiveness, and discrimination. Secretiveness is the norm.

Sun in Scorpio

The Sun in Scorpio person is intense. You never approach anything half-heartedly, and your passion inspires others to follow in your path. A born strategist, you know when to charge forward and when to pull back. You shine in a crisis, displaying a calm demeanor, clear thinking, and a take-charge attitude. Your ability to uncover secrets and get to the bottom of things makes you a good detective, investigator, or researcher.

Moon in Scorpio

The Moon in Scorpio person is secretive. Emotionally intense, you may struggle with your feelings and strive to be impartial. Your passion for life helps you go after what you want with great success. Rarely on the sidelines, you prefer to create your own opportunities. Shrewd and perceptive, you can motivate others and effect change. You are at your best when you channel your strong emotions toward helping others.

Mercury in Scorpio

The Mercury in Scorpio person is incisive. Your mind is quick to assess and evaluate the situation, giving you the tactical advantage. You can sense others' weaknesses and use this information to help or hinder—here is the healer or military strategist. Secretive, you rarely speak about personal matters but can find out anything there is to know about someone else. You can be an excellent researcher, detective, or investigator.

Venus in Scorpio

The Venus in Scorpio person is ardent. Your passion and magnetism are attractive to the opposite sex, though you can exercise restraint at will. You may be drawn to people who make their own rules or whom society considers scoundrels. Strong feelings can surface in your love relationships, and you insist on total commitment. Creative and intense, you can focus your considerable talents on the healing arts.

Mars in Scorpio

The Mars in Scorpio person is eager. You approach your goals with a strong commitment and an all-or-nothing attitude. Instinctive and perceptive, you can use your considerable power to heal others. You make your presence felt even when you do nothing at all—just by showing up. Your passion and strong will enable you to conquer anything you desire; however, temperance allows you to succeed.

Jupiter in Scorpio

The Jupiter in Scorpio person is profound. You have an aptitude for finance, and good judgment and intuition can help you succeed with investment strategies. You can be lucky in the financial markets and in overseeing the assets of others. Your interest in uncovering truth makes you a good researcher or student of the mystery schools. You may be interested in writing thrillers, detective stories, or crime novels.

Saturn in Scorpio

The Saturn in Scorpio person is determined. Your resourcefulness, combined with shrewdness, enables you to succeed in business where others might fail. Perceptive and even psychic, you are a good judge of character and can evaluate people based on your instincts. You have a strong desire for material wealth, and your single-mindedness makes this possible. As you reach your goals, you can bring others along to share the rewards.

Uranus in Scorpio

The Uranus in Scorpio person is astute. Your penetrating insight enables you to see beyond the obvious to what lies beneath the surface. As a result, you may counsel or assist others in solving their problems. Unique vision and depth of understanding may help you come up with new ways to solve mysteries. When your creative passions are positively channeled, you can find cures, make discoveries, or answer age-old questions.

Neptune in Scorpio

The Neptune in Scorpio person is insightful. Since Neptune remains in a sign for fourteen years, it influences an entire generation. It was last in Scorpio from 1957 to 1970, when drug use became a national issue. If you were born with Neptune in Scorpio, you may be interested in medical research or the mysteries of the universe. You will likely have a strong attraction to psychic phenomena.

Pluto in Scorpio

The Pluto in Scorpio person is powerful. Pluto moves slowly and has an irregular orbit, remaining in a sign for anywhere from twelve to twenty-two years. It therefore influences an entire generation. Pluto was last in Scorpio from 1984 to 1995 and will not be there again until the next century. This is the generation that will make medical breakthroughs, find cures, and even create new life through artificial means.

Planets in Sagittarius ♐

Any planet in Sagittarius will behave with confidence and have an adventurous air. Among the qualities associated with this mutable fire sign are fairness, directness, and curiosity. Candor can be problematic if overemphasized.

Sun in Sagittarius

The Sun is Sagittarius person is direct. Refreshingly honest, you can get into trouble because not everyone appreciates your openness, especially if they see it as tactless. Your adventurous nature keeps you on the go, always looking for something new to explore. When things become routine or stagnant, you are easily bored. The best way to avoid that is to live life to the fullest—something you really know how to do.

Moon in Sagittarius

The Moon in Sagittarius person is restless. Your optimism and friendly attitude help you maintain a positive outlook on life. You enjoy feeling free to roam and expect to be given considerable latitude in your relationships. Emotionally uninhibited, you can express feelings with openness and honesty. Your sense of adventure and joy for life keep you young well beyond your years.

Mercury in Sagittarius

The Mercury in Sagittarius person is broad-minded. Your directness can catch people off-guard because you are apt to say exactly what's on your mind. Idealistic and farsighted, you can grasp the big picture, though you have less patience with the details. Your curiosity and perception are acute, and you may prefer to ponder the mysteries of the universe or other expansive topics.

Venus in Sagittarius

The Venus in Sagittarius person is generous. Lighthearted, outgoing, and adventurous, you attract many friends and acquaintances but prefer not to get tied down. You may be looking for the ideal love, which rarely exists outside of oneself. You can have more than a passing interest in speculation or high-risk ventures. Conversely, you may pursue a spiritual path or one in which you can share your wisdom with others.

Mars in Sagittarius

The Mars in Sagittarius person is adventurous. When your interest is peaked, energy follows; otherwise, you get bored and cannot sustain the momentum. Independent and restless, you will not tolerate restrictions or confinement of any kind. Your sense of adventure may have you traveling the globe or at least exploring through books. You can do well in sports or any activity that provides a lot of physical movement.

Jupiter in Sagittarius

The Jupiter in Sagittarius person is magnanimous. Your great love of freedom and independence is paramount, and though you may settle down, you will never be tied down. You can be lucky in obtaining rewards like a scholarship, endowment, or grant. Your confidence and willingness to take risks can lead to financial success, but you have to manage a tendency to squander what you have gained.

Saturn in Sagittarius

The Saturn in Sagittarius person is honorable. Your open and honest nature, though admirable, is not always practical because you can be too forthcoming. You approach your objectives by learning all you can about the subject at hand before making a decision. You have lofty goals and may do well in business, science, education, or law. You can be fearless when it comes to standing up for what you believe in.

Uranus in Sagittarius

The Uranus in Sagittarius person is intellectual. Willing to draw attention to needed reform, you are guided by your good judgment and principles. Innovative and farsighted, your views on many subjects, including religion, can be ahead of their time. You want to expand your horizons and may travel extensively or explore new concepts. You may be interested in legal reform, and your insights can stir things up.

Neptune in Sagittarius

The Neptune in Sagittarius person is faithful. Since Neptune remains in a sign for fourteen years, it influences an entire generation. It was last in Sagittarius from 1971 to 1985. Those born with Neptune in Sagittarius are part of a generation that may begin the process of redefining religious and spiritual principles. Perhaps the rigidity of orthodox faiths will dissolve into spiritual oneness.

Pluto in Sagittarius

Pluto moves slowly and has an irregular orbit, remaining in a sign for anywhere from twelve to twenty-two years. It therefore influences an entire generation. Pluto moved into Sagittarius in 1995 and will remain there until 2008. Those born with Pluto in Sagittarius are part of a generation that may be active in bringing about educational and legal reform. Exploration of outer space is a probability.

Planets in Capricorn ♑

Any planet in Capricorn will operate in a deliberate manner and show a steady determination. Among the qualities associated with this cardinal earth sign are dependability, prudence, and discipline. There is a serious demeanor.

Sun in Capricorn

The Sun in Capricorn person is resourceful. Once you set your sights on something, your resolve is unmatched and the achievement of your goals is inevitable. Your leadership qualities make for success in business and gain you a reputation for being honest and dependable. It's not unusual for you to make long-range plans because you expect it will take a while before you reach the top of the mountain. You are happiest when you have something to strive for.

Moon in Capricorn

The Moon in Capricorn person is dependable. You may be an efficiency expert, capable of finding the best way to get the job done. Though you can appear aloof, you are just as sensitive as anyone else, preferring to hide your emotions rather than reveal them. You may feel secure only when you take control of your circumstances. In time, your patience is rewarded, and you will get the recognition and acknowledgement you deserve.

Mercury in Capricorn

The Mercury in Capricorn person is focused. Your concentration level, attention to detail, and good memory are enviable and are all qualities that lend themselves to scientific research. Earnest and resolute, you learn your subject inside out before offering an opinion. Committed to excellence, you may do well in a service-oriented business of your own. Your serious demeanor and speech give you an air of wisdom beyond your years.

Venus in Capricorn

The Venus in Capricorn person is cautious. Your reserve in matters of the heart may stem from a desire to shield yourself from disappointment. When you make a commitment, it is a serious matter and is often with someone who can improve your status. You approach love in a practical manner, evaluating the benefits of a partnership much in the same way as you would a business relationship.

Mars in Capricorn

The Mars in Capricorn person is conscientious. Your determination and ability to work toward a goal with persistence ensure a successful outcome. Capable of taking on responsibility, you can do well in many fields, but business management may be a good fit. You are self-reliant and proud, rarely offering an explanation for your actions. Your stamina and endurance keep you going long after others have quit.

Jupiter in Capricorn

The Jupiter in Capricorn person is ethical. You are conscientious and disciplined in the pursuit of objectives, making for good business decisions. Concerned with basics, you're able to see how to reduce waste and get the most for dollars spent. Your new initiatives are well planned so that you can make steady progress. Some might consider you too cautious, but your prudence and good judgment win in the end.

Saturn in Capricorn

The Saturn in Capricorn person is determined. Your practical view of the world keeps you grounded as you work toward achieving your goals. Efficient and discerning, you can see things clearly and stay a step ahead of the competition. A take-charge individual, you are ambitious and don't mind assuming responsibility. You are not one to back away from obligations and will go the extra mile to get the job done.

Uranus in Capricorn

The Uranus in Capricorn person is pragmatic. You can introduce a unique approach to an old way of doing things that is like a breath of fresh air. With insight and inventiveness, you can change conventional thinking on an array of subjects. The changes you suggest can be both practical and highly developed, perhaps in the technological field. You may contribute to new breakthroughs in science and governmental reform.

Neptune in Capricorn

The Neptune in Capricorn person is compliant. Since Neptune remains in a sign for fourteen years, it influences an entire generation. It was last in Capricorn from 1984 to 1998. Those born with Neptune in Capricorn are part of a generation that will be faced with environmental issues. They most likely will address the problems of Earth pollution and global warming. Government corruption is another likely target.

Pluto in Capricorn

Pluto moves slowly and has an irregular orbit, remaining in a sign for anywhere from twelve to twenty-two years. It therefore influences an entire generation. Since Pluto was not discovered until 1930, we have not observed it in Capricorn since its discovery. However, it was in Capricorn in the mid to late 1700s during the time of the American Revolution. Pluto will next be in Capricorn at the end of 2008. We can only speculate as to how it will influence the next generation. The likely subjects to be addressed are government reform and environmental issues.

Planets in Aquarius ≈

Any planet in Aquarius will show an air of eccentricity, individuality, and uniqueness. Among the qualities associated with this fixed air sign are imagination, insight, and inventiveness. A rebellious streak may be evident.

Sun in Aquarius

The Sun in Aquarius person is futuristic. Your way of seeing things is often far ahead of current trends, so much so that you may be considered a visionary. Friendships mean a great deal to you and may even surpass family relationships. You can be eccentric, unconventional, intellectual, or zany, but never ordinary. An inventive side is often evident, and you may have more than a few patents pending.

Moon in Aquarius

The Moon in Aquarius person is impersonal. Your independence and freedom-loving nature may give the impression that you are emotionally detached. Actually, you can nurture and love someone while giving him or her plenty of breathing room. You need lots of stimuli to keep from getting bored and may busy yourself with new studies on a variety of subjects. Being on the go is appealing, and you may travel often to alleviate feelings of restlessness.

Mercury in Aquarius

The Mercury in Aquarius person is resourceful. Imaginative and innovative, you have many creative ideas about how to do things more efficiently. Flashes of insight may seem to come from nowhere, and the quicker you get your thoughts on paper, the better. Your keen intuition and quick assessment of the situation enable you to avert problems before they happen. Processing information at warp speed is easy—conveying it may be a bit more difficult.

Venus in Aquarius

The Venus in Aquarius person is playful. You embrace friends and acquaintances easily but may be more restrained in intimate relationships.

Friendship first and then love can prove to be more satisfying. Humanitarian at heart, you prefer to be part of a bigger plan, group, or organization with a purpose. You are interested in people and eager to stir things up in a way that can elevate, inspire, and educate them.

Mars in Aquarius

The Mars in Aquarius person is inventive. Your independence and enterprising nature keep you from work that is routine; you prefer to pursue an unconventional course of endeavor. Your power is focused through the intellect, and you may write science fiction or be interested in technological research. You may have an aptitude for competitive board games, backgammon, chess, or word games. Uniquely creative, you can turn an unusual hobby into something productive.

Jupiter in Aquarius

The Jupiter in Aquarius person is ingenious. You're interested in exploring creative new ideas, wherever they may take you. An open-minded attitude about religion and spirituality lets you embrace people of all faiths. It's in your nature to get along with everyone, and you may enjoy working on group projects. You have a way with people, and they willingly follow your lead. Your talent for innovation can open doors in the field of scientific research.

Saturn in Aquarius

The Saturn in Aquarius person is clever. Friends are important to most people, but to you, they are family and assume an important role in your life. You can be creative and innovative in business and will gain the respect of your peers. Your strength of character enables you to take on a great deal of responsibility. You can make breakthroughs in many areas by approaching old problems in new and creative ways.

Uranus in Aquarius

The Uranus in Aquarius person is visionary. You like to turn things inside out and upside down to create a better way of doing something. Your intellectual mind may lean toward new technology or science, and you can make contributions in those fields. Inventive and original, you are likely to go your own way in whatever you do. You can be impatient when others are slow to see what is so clear to you. You're always ahead of your time.

Neptune in Aquarius

The Neptune in Aquarius person is humanitarian. Since Neptune remains in a sign for fourteen years, it influences an entire generation. It moved into Aquarius in late 1998 and will remain there until the year 2012. Those born with Neptune in Aquarius may be a generation of futurists who dream of exploring the universe. They are likely to sacrifice for an ideal. In the words of *Star Trek's* Mr. Spock: "The needs of the many outweigh the needs of the few or the one."

Pluto in Aquarius

Pluto moves slowly and has an irregular orbit, remaining in a sign for anywhere from twelve to twenty-two years. It therefore influences an entire generation. Since Pluto was not discovered until 1930, we have not observed it in Aquarius since its discovery. However, it was in Aquarius in the late 1700s at the time of the French Revolution. The struggle that shook Europe to its foundations was based on the desire for liberty and equality—Aquarian principles. Pluto will not move into Aquarius again until 2024.

Planets in Pisces ♓

Any planet in Pisces will display gentle, compassionate, and kind behavior. Among the qualities associated with this mutable water sign are intuition, patience, and humility. Dreaminess and a tendency to be reclusive will be evident.

Sun in Pisces

The Sun in Pisces person is compassionate. Introspective and in tune with your surroundings, you may need to retreat and spend time alone to maintain your equilibrium. You can create a world of illusion through art, film, or photography. An ability to fantasize and let your imagination run wild can find expression in many forms; animation is one possibility. Charitable in nature, you readily help those in need.

Moon in Pisces

The Moon in Pisces person is gentle. Acquiescent, agreeable, and sensitive, you desire peace and value serenity above all else. With an emotional makeup that is only contented through divine inspiration, you may find worldly endeavors lacking. You have great sympathy for people who are disadvantaged and will go far to help someone in need. Your heightened sensitivity may find expression in music, art, or other creative forms.

Mercury in Pisces

The Mercury in Pisces person is imaginative. Your mental process is more psychic and intuitive than logical and cerebral. This is not to say that one approach is better than the other; they're just different. You can express your sensitivity through the written word, perhaps through poetry or musical composition, for instance. Your heightened sensitivity opens you up to the environment; you should surround yourself with positive people and things.

Venus in Pisces

The Venus in Pisces person is idealistic. Your compassionate and loving nature may incline you toward self-sacrifice, but victimization is not recommended. You can accomplish a lot when focused on helping those who are disadvantaged, as long as they want to help themselves. You may be gifted with musical or artistic talent. Highly emotional and sensitive, you can express your feelings through many creative outlets. Photography is one possibility.

Mars in Pisces

The Mars in Pisces person is charitable. An energetic imagination may help you create beautiful imagery that can be expressed through different art forms. Many musicians have this placement. You may actively pursue a spiritual path, preferring to achieve enlightenment rather than worldly goals. Your empathy and understanding may be directed toward helping others who are sick, poor, or neglected.

Jupiter in Pisces

The Jupiter in Pisces person is inspired. Your interest in quietly helping others may earn you the title of Good Samaritan. Your boundless imagination can find expression through music or other art forms. You may pursue liberal arts or the humanities and have an interest in spiritual or metaphysical studies. Your sensitivity can give you heightened perception, with which you may develop psychic talents such as clairvoyance or clairaudience.

Saturn in Pisces

The Saturn in Pisces person is tolerant. Your goals tend to be less structured because you prefer to go with the flow, so to speak. When you trust your intuition, it guides you toward your objectives, even if you don't have a specific plan. Your compassion toward others is commendable, and you can even go too far in helping the underdog. You may have a talent for acting, performing, or directing motion pictures.

Uranus in Pisces

The Uranus in Pisces person is intuitive. A very keen psychic awareness may produce visions, prophetic dreams, or other extrasensory experiences. You may have an interest in serving humanity and using your talents in this vein. Genius and imagination can come together with this placement. Creativity can be extraordinary, as it was in the life of Judy Garland, born in 1922 when Uranus was last in Pisces.

Neptune in Pisces

The Neptune in Pisces person is empathetic. Since Neptune remains in a sign for fourteen years, it influences an entire generation. It will move into Pisces in 2011, where it will be in dignity in its own sign—meaning it will be strong. At the same time, Pluto will be transiting Capricorn. This combination may give us a generation of idealists; they may be equally determined to make those in power accountable for their actions.

Pluto in Pisces

Pluto moves slowly and has an irregular orbit, remaining in a sign for anywhere from twelve to twenty-two years. It therefore influences an entire generation. Since Pluto was not discovered until 1930, we have not observed it in Pisces since its discovery. However, it was in Pisces during the first two decades of the 1800s. It will not be in Pisces again until 2043.

chapter six

THE ASPECTS

An aspect is a contact between two planets or between a planet and a point in your horoscope. When there is contact, the planets work together. These contacts are measured in degrees and form angular relationships. All you need to know about aspects is which planets in your horoscope are connected in this way. The following chapter will define the meanings of the aspects made by the ten planets. You will be able to identify which planets in your horoscope are connected in this way by locating the symbol in the aspect grid. The aspect grid usually appears below your horoscope wheel on the printout of your birth chart, as shown on the next page. It shows which planets and points are connected in this way. The symbols for the five major aspects are as follows:

Symbol	Name	Measurement
☌	Conjunction	0 degrees
✶	Sextile	60 degrees
□	Square	90 degrees
△	Trine	120 degrees
☍	Opposition	180 degrees

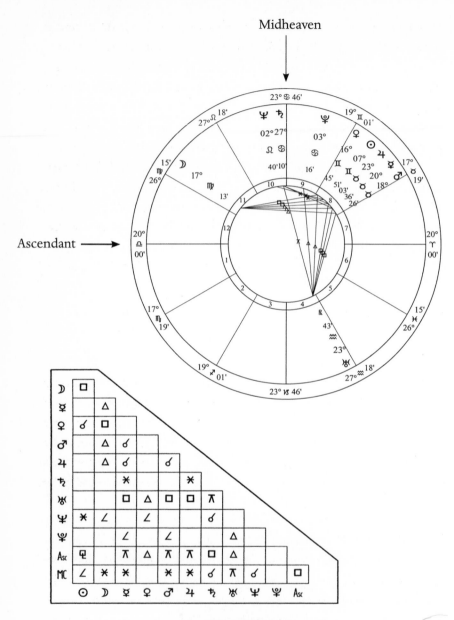

John Fitzgerald Kennedy
May 29, 1917 / 3:00 p.m. EST / Brookline, Massachusetts
Placidus Houses

Whatever the aspects between planets, there is always the potential to work with the energies in a positive way. Aspects are termed *harmonious* (☌ ✶ △) or *stressful* (□ ☍), but this is only terminology. It is always your choice as to how to express your energy and direct your thoughts. You are the master of your universe.

When a planet aspects the Ascendant, your personality will reflect qualities of that planet, while any planet that aspects the Midheaven can influence your choice of career, vocation, or work. Often the planet making the closest aspect to the Midheaven is the strongest career indicator.

An aspect has an *orb of influence*, which is the range within which an aspect is considered effective. This range is usually a few degrees within the defined distance. For example, though a sextile is defined as 60° between two points, the allowed range is between 55° and 65°, or five degrees on either side of exactitude.

♇ PLUTO ASPECTS

Pluto-Sun

The more harmonious aspects (☌ ✶ △) will endow you with a strong identity and often an ability to heal others. You are someone whom people take notice of and either like immediately or the complete opposite. Powerful and intense, you can take charge and prefer to be self-employed. A born detective, you ferret out information better than anyone. With the more stressful aspects (□ ☍), you may have difficulty with authority.

Pluto-Moon

The more harmonious aspects (☌ ✶ △) bestow an emotional intensity toward everything. You are passionate and either love powerfully or the complete opposite. Your feelings are never mild, because you feel things deeply. Women in your life can be strong-willed and somewhat unpredictable. With the more stressful aspects (□ ☍), you may have female friends who are envious or suddenly disappear from your life.

Pluto-Mercury

A persuasive ability is inherent with this combination, and with the more harmonious aspects (σ ✳ △), you can be an excellent salesperson, therapist, psychiatrist, or mystery writer. Whatever you put into words—verbal or written—has staying power. Your mind probes deeply to find answers to questions, and you can be an excellent researcher. The more stressful aspects (□ ☍) tend to give an intensity of speech.

Pluto-Venus

You love with intensity regardless of the aspect between Pluto and Venus. The more harmonious aspects (σ ✳ △) can indicate creativity and inspiration. Your relationships are a dominant theme in your life because you are not happy without one. You may be passionate in your pursuit of a partner and dismissive if rejected. The stressful aspects (□ ☍) may suggest the need to work out anger toward loved ones.

Pluto-Mars

Your powerful energy can be aimed at a career in the military or secret service. The more harmonious aspects (σ ✳ △) show potent, directed action focused on positive endeavors. You like anything that presents a challenge and is worth fighting for. You may be a surgeon, attorney, or negotiator. With the more stressful aspects (□ ☍), you may be inclined toward sports and other competitive fields.

Pluto-Jupiter

You form your own ideology and values, rarely accepting what others have taught you. The harmonious aspects (σ ✳ △) show a serious, penetrating assessment of higher principles like philosophy, law, and religion. Your wisdom and keen awareness can influence others. You may choose a vocation in which you can counsel or teach. The more stressful aspects (□ ☍) may cause you to challenge lofty ideas.

Pluto-Saturn

You are less concerned with maintaining appearances than with eliminating what isn't working. With the harmonious aspects (σ ✳ △), you tend to charge right in and take on responsibilities. You can run a tight ship and do whatever is required to get the job done. With the more stressful aspects (□ ☍), you may be inclined to challenge old standards or government bureaucracies.

Pluto-Uranus

You can focus your power on doing things differently and making positive changes as needed. With the harmonious aspects (☌ ✶ △), you have the vision and insight to improve upon existing conditions and implement creative solutions. You may find the technological revolution a good fit, as it is both stimulating and challenging. With the more stressful aspects (□ ☍), you have the urge to stir things up.

Pluto-Neptune

You are in search of an ideal or the deeper meaning of life. With the harmonious aspects (☌ ✶ △), you may have prophetic dreams or the ability to tap into the nonphysical realms. A fertile imagination can be expressed through music or other creative art forms. You may discover true spirituality as opposed to dogma. With the stressful aspects (□ ☍), you can deceive yourself or avoid reality.

Pluto-Ascendant

You have the ability to convey your powerful thoughts without saying much—just a glance will do. With the harmonious aspects (☌ ✶ △), you are likely to find challenges stimulating. Your determination and staying power help you achieve your goals. You just don't give up unless you want to. With the stressful aspects (□ ☍), you can be pushy or inflexible.

Pluto-Midheaven

Your career goals are ambitious, and you will take matters into your own hands. With the harmonious aspects (☌ ✶ △), you succeed by your own standards and prefer to be self-employed. Money management, medicine, demolition, and construction are some career possibilities.

The more stressful aspects (□ ☍) may encourage a high-risk occupation such as venture capitalist or demolition expert.

♆ NEPTUNE ASPECTS

Neptune-Sun

You can be a dreamer, but your dreams are glorious, romantic, and idealistic. With the harmonious aspects (☌ ⚹ △), you can do well in any creative field. You have a good imagination, refinement, and great sensitivity. Drawn to helping others, you may be a healer. With the more stressful aspects (□ ☍), you may have a savior mentality or poor self-esteem or attract those who take advantage.

Neptune-Moon

Impressionable and emotionally very sensitive, you can be a wonderful musician. With the harmonious aspects (☌ ⚹ △), you are imaginative, creative, and intuitive. Keenly psychic, you soak up your surroundings and need to be in a peaceful setting. With the stressful aspects (□ ☍), you may overreact, daydream, or develop avoidance tactics. People with problems can drain you emotionally.

Neptune-Mercury

Your imagery can be inspired and find expression in poetry, musical composition, or other creative outlets. With the harmonious aspects (☌ ⚹ △), you may have mystical or extrasensory impressions that are valid and visionary. Though idealistic, you can use this quality constructively, with an eye toward helping others. With the more stressful aspects (□ ☍), you may lack concentration or be a dreamer.

Neptune-Venus

A true romantic, you have a gentle nature and may dream of ideal love and finding a soul mate. With the harmonious aspects (☌ ⚹ △), your loving and caring nature is extended to all unconditionally. You may have musical talent, good taste, and a refined sense of style. Spiritually inclined, you may wish to live a holy life; this is even more of a possibility with the stressful aspects (□ ☍). You may relinquish personal love for universal love.

Neptune-Mars

Your charisma is unmistakable, and others may find it difficult to decline your requests. The more positive aspects (☌ ⚹ △) endow you with compassion, intuition, and a strong inclination toward selfless service. You may be drawn to oceanography or other aspects of ocean science. Stillness and serenity may be appealing. With the more stressful aspects (□ ☍), you need to be selective in choosing your companions.

Neptune-Jupiter

Your interest in fair play goes beyond the norm, and you may be willing to make personal sacrifices to put right an injustice. The more positive aspects (☌ ⚹ △) enhance the imagination, and your expansive dreams can become a reality. Your openness and accessibility attract benefits from many different sources. With the more stressful aspects (□ ☍), you may over-idealize and open yourself to disappointment.

Neptune-Saturn

The more positive aspects (☌ ⚹ △) tend to balance both the practical and creative aspects of your personality, and you can actualize your dreams. You may rely on your natural intuition to guide you toward sound business decisions. Your sensitivity and reason may help you assist others who have less clarity. The more stressful aspects (□ ☍) can mean that you worry needlessly about things that are not all that problematic.

Neptune-Uranus

Aspects between these two planets—when they occur—will be in effect for many years, influencing an entire generation. The more positive aspects (☌ ⚹ △) may introduce forward-thinking individuals who dream of a better world. With the more stressful aspects (□ ☍), we may see a generation of idealists who want radical change no matter what the cost.

Neptune-Ascendant

Very sensitive both emotionally and physically, you can perceive what others are feeling. The positive aspects (☌ ✳ △), especially the conjunction, can give you a Piscean personality—always willing to do things for others. Your tolerance for unpleasantness is quite low, and you may prefer to isolate yourself from anything disagreeable. With the more stressful aspects (□ ☍), avoid alcohol and drugs as a means of escape.

Neptune-Midheaven

With the positive aspects (☌ ✳ △), your creative and artistic talents are most likely to play a role in career choices. You may be drawn to the arts, film, music, dance, design, or photography. Neptune also rules the sea, so oceanography or marine biology are strong possibilities. Other career choices may include medicine and, especially with the more stressful aspects (□ ☍), caring for those who are poor or disadvantaged.

♅ URANUS ASPECTS

Uranus-Sun

A measure of genius describes the person with Uranus in aspect to the Sun. The more positive aspects (☌ ✳ △) give originality, inventiveness, and independence. You can do things differently and even have strokes of brilliance. Your magnetic personality captivates the opposite sex. With the more stressful aspects (□ ☍), you may delight in shocking others.

Uranus-Moon

Your restless nature may keep you on the move, always looking for the newest and latest advances in all areas. The more positive aspects (☌ ✳ △) endow you with a magnetic personality, strong intuition, and good intellect. You are always willing to break with convention and try something new. With the more stressful aspects (□ ☍), you can be impetuous or spontaneous—it's your choice.

Uranus-Mercury

Your mind is focused on cutting-edge technology or revolutionary ideas. Your intuition, sharp intellect, and flashes of pure genius are evident, especially with the more positive aspects (♂ ✶ △). Progressive thinking often can result in concepts that are ahead of their time. With the more stressful aspects (□ ♂°), you may be fixed in your thinking or impatient with those who are less original.

Uranus-Venus

Though you want a relationship just as much as the next person, it's important for you to have complete autonomy for a lasting union. Your taste is unique, and personal magnetism is strong, especially with the more positive aspects (♂ ✶ △). You may have rare artistic talent and can attract money through original creative endeavors. With the more stressful aspects (□ ♂°), you may change partners frequently.

Uranus-Mars

You like to take risks and will follow your own path, regardless of what others think. Your courage, vitality, and persistence are emphasized, especially with the more positive aspects (♂ ✶ △). Anything new and high-tech will appeal to you. Boredom is the only intolerable condition, so you pursue adventure with abandon. The more stressful aspects (□ ♂°) can indicate a tendency to be accident-prone.

Uranus-Jupiter

You may be attracted to concepts and ideas that are unconventional, ahead of their time, or far-reaching, like quantum physics, for example. Your grasp of broad principles gives you a futuristic ideology, especially with the more positive aspects (♂ ✶ △). Unusual interests promise an interesting life, and you have spiritual awareness. With the more stressful aspects (□ ♂°), your liberal outlook can be considered eccentric.

Uranus-Saturn

A unique blend of practicality and innovation can help you find new approaches to solving existing problems. You are your own best counsel and may be self-taught on many subjects, especially with the more positive aspects (☌ ⚹ △). Career goals may focus on the broadcasting fields, journalism, or the sciences. The more stressful aspects (□ ☍) can indicate conflict with authority.

Uranus-Ascendant

You can exhibit an independent, somewhat unusual personality and have unique interests, like astrology, for example. The positive aspects (☌ ⚹ △), especially the conjunction, can give you Aquarian-like traits—eccentric, friendly, and magnetic. You may have a strong desire to help others or to get involved with humanitarian causes. The stressful aspects (□ ☍) can indicate a rebellious nature or trouble with partners.

Uranus-Midheaven

Your occupation has to be exciting and offer variety to be lasting. You may be better off self-employed. With the positive aspects (☌ ⚹ △), especially the conjunction, your unique vision and insight can be expressed through your profession. You may be an innovative astrologer, television or radio personality, or technology expert. With the stressful aspects (□ ☍), you can have problems with employers and superiors.

♄ SATURN ASPECTS

Saturn-Sun

With strength and persistence, you can accomplish a great deal once you set your sights on something. Through discipline and hard work, you eventually receive recognition, though it may be delayed. You are not one to shrug off responsibility, especially with the positive aspects (☌ ⚹ △). With the more stressful aspects (□ ☍), you may be easily discouraged or frustrated and inclined to give up the challenge.

Saturn-Moon

Responsible and practical, you may do well with real estate investment and business in general. You enjoy your alone time, especially with the more positive aspects (☌ ✶ △), and can spend hours immersed in your work. You are happy with the simple things in life and may shun extravagance. With the more stressful aspects (☐ ☍), you may feel burdened with responsibility and need to lighten up a bit.

Saturn-Mercury

Not one to make small talk, you prefer to speak only when you have something meaningful to say. The positive aspects (☌ ✶ △) enhance a good memory, strong reasoning, and practicality. You may be a natural educator, advisor, or counselor. To avoid mistakes, you prefer to think things through before making a decision. With the stressful aspects (☐ ☍), you strive to overcome negative thinking.

Saturn-Venus

Your loyalty and commitment to those you love are unequaled, and you can attract lasting relationships. You may prefer older or more mature partners. With the positive aspects (☌ ✶ △), a strong sense of responsibility can help you achieve financial success. Your discipline helps you successfully manage resources. With the more stressful aspects (☐ ☍), you may feel that you have to work hard and push yourself to earn every penny.

Saturn-Mars

Good judgment, discipline, and practical planning can help you achieve your ambitions with the positive aspects (☌ ✶ △) between these two planets. You can pace yourself and sustain your actions over the long term. Your willingness to work hard for what you want can result in business success. With the more stressful aspects (☐ ☍), you may be worried about failure and therefore refuse to try.

Saturn-Jupiter

You can balance the practical, ambitious side of your nature with the more philosophical side, resulting in success in your chosen field, especially in business. Your broad interests and work ethic result in accomplishments in many different areas, especially with the positive aspects

(σ $*$ $\triangle$) between these two planets. The more stressful aspects ($\square$ σ^{o}) can put a damper on your self-confidence.

Saturn-Ascendant

With the conjunction, you may exhibit Capricorn personality traits no matter what your Ascendant sign; thus, you appear cautious, disciplined, and serious. Overall, the positive aspects (σ $*$ $\triangle$) suggest an ability to stay the course and, with hard work and patience, accomplish what you want. With the stressful aspects ($\square$ σ^{o}), your accomplishments can depend on your willingness to accept responsibilities.

Saturn-Midheaven

Organized, practical, and persistent, the positive aspects (σ $*$ $\triangle$) almost always result in success in your chosen career or vocation. Even the stressful aspects ($\square$ σ^{o}) can provide the drive and ambition to succeed, but it may take a while longer. You can succeed in your own business or in the corporate world. You will not give up the goal no matter how long it takes; sheer determination gets you there.

♃ JUPITER ASPECTS

Jupiter-Sun

With the positive aspects (σ $*$ $\triangle$) between Jupiter and the Sun, a sense of optimism colors your life, and you can be fortunate or lucky in many ways. Your willingness to explore new possibilities can lead to opportunity and financial success. A can-do attitude helps you navigate around obstacles to come out on top. With the stressful aspects ($\square$ σ^{o}), you may be extravagant or lack discipline.

Jupiter-Moon

A generous heart and inner optimism help you attract many benefits into your life with the positive aspects (σ $*$ $\triangle$) between Jupiter and the Moon. Your love of people and desire to interact with them enable you succeed in the public sector. You benefit from public support, recognition, or honors. With the more stressful aspects (□ ♂°), you may be overindulgent or too sensitive.

Jupiter-Mercury

Your can grasp the big picture and analyze details with equal finesse when Jupiter and Mercury are in good aspect (♂ ✳ △). With a positive attitude, you can stay focused on the results you want and give no attention whatsoever to failure. Perceptive and keenly observant, you can do well in the medical or legal field. With the stressful aspects (□ ♂°), you can be impulsive or overconfident.

Jupiter-Venus

Refined and compassionate, you have a benevolent nature that attracts equal benefits from others when Jupiter and Venus are in good aspect (♂ ✳ △). Your strong faith and positive expectations can help you create wealth and success in your life. Sensitive and kind, you may allow others to impose upon you. With the more stressful aspects (□ ♂°), you can be wasteful and may have to learn how to say no.

Jupiter-Mars

Your sense of justice drives you to fight for a good cause, and you may be inclined to study law. The positive aspects (♂ ✳ △) enhance optimism, energy, and athletic ability. Straightforward and persistent, you follow the rules and can achieve what you want through your own efforts. With the stressful aspects (□ ♂°), you can be reckless and tend to undermine yourself.

Jupiter-Ascendant

An optimistic attitude prevails with the positive aspects from Jupiter to the Ascendant (♂ ✳ △). The conjunction will add Sagittarian traits to your personality, so a sense of adventure permeates your life. You enjoy your freedom to come and go and may travel extensively and be interested in a variety of subjects. With the more stressful aspects (□ ♂°), you may have a tendency to put on weight.

Jupiter-Midheaven

With the positive Jupiter aspects (☌ ✶ △) to the Midheaven, luck plays a role in the achievement of your career goals. Even the more stressful Jupiter aspects (□ ☍) can help you attain your goals, because they increase opportunities and give you confidence. Career choices are varied and may include the travel business, show business, publishing, writing, banking, and international law.

♂ MARS ASPECTS

Mars-Sun

Your energy is never-ending, especially with the conjunction, and you have the courage to take risks. With the more positive aspects (☌ ✶ △), you can be more than a little impulsive but better able to control your actions. You can successfully go after what you want and need to be on the go to be happy. With the more stressful aspects (□ ☍), you can be too hasty or aggressive.

Mars-Moon

A powerful imagination and strong intuition enable you to be creative and stay ahead of current trends. With the positive aspects between Mars and the Moon (☌ ✶ △), you can work well in the public eye or tap into public consciousness. You feel with intensity and know when to assert yourself and when to back away. With the stressful aspects (□ ☍), you may allow your emotions to overrule your judgment.

Mars-Mercury

Not afraid to state your opinions, you can be quite courageous in taking on those with whom you disagree. With the positive aspects between Mars and Mercury (☌ ✶ △), your mind is sharp and you can debate with the best of them. You tend to attack problems and waste little time in analyzing the cause. With the more stressful aspects (□ ☍), you may be argumentative.

Mars-Venus

You are highly creative, charming, and more than a little attractive to the opposite sex. The positive aspects between Mars and Venus (♂ ✶ △) enhance the pleasure side of life. You can attract both money and a happy, well-balanced relationship. You may have more than a casual interest in the arts and can be a prolific artist. With the stressful aspects (□ ♂), you can blow hot and cold when it comes to love.

Mars-Ascendant

An energetic, assertive attitude is apparent with the positive aspects from Mars to the Ascendant (♂ ✶ △). The conjunction will give Aries traits to your personality, so you may be impatient and eager to be first in whatever you do. Enthusiastic and sure of yourself, you can motivate others into action. With the more stressful aspects (□ ♂), you may have to manage an aggressive nature.

Mars-Midheaven

With the positive Mars aspects to the Midheaven (♂ ✶ △), career choices are varied as long as there is an element of excitement, challenge or new initiatives to keep you satisfied. Anything from counseling to a military career is possible. With the more stressful aspects (□ ♂), you may be better off working for yourself because there is the likelihood of conflicts with superiors and employers.

♀ VENUS ASPECTS

Venus-Sun

Venus never travels very far from the Sun; therefore, its only major aspect is a conjunction to the Sun. If you have the conjunction (♂), you may be charming, affectionate, and good-natured. Your artistic talents can be enhanced, as well as your sense of style. You will most likely enjoy all the finer things in life—good food, fashionable clothes, beautiful collectibles, and good company.

Venus-Moon

You feel right at home when surrounded with beautiful things. The positive aspects between Venus and the Moon (♂ ✳ △) enhance your desire for the best money can buy. Your innate charm and sensuality are attractive to the opposite sex, though you may not be aware of how you affect people. With the stressful aspects (□ ♂°), you may have to give your all in personal relationships before receiving in kind.

Venus-Mercury

Mercury never travels very far from the Sun or Venus; therefore, the only major aspects between Venus and Mercury are a conjunction or sextile (♂ ✳). If you have either aspect, your social skills are refined and you may have musical or artistic talents. Friendly and outgoing, you are a people person who enjoys interacting with others. They find your manner charming, gracious, and polished.

Venus-Ascendant

With the positive Venus aspects to the Ascendant (♂ ✳ △), especially the conjunction, you are attractive. You may exhibit traits of both Libra and, to a lesser extent, Taurus; sociability and sensibility will be strong components of your personality. Naturally charming, you can finesse people into going along with your desires. With the more stressful aspects (□ ♂°), you can be self-indulgent and wasteful, especially with money.

Venus-Midheaven

With the positive Venus aspects to the Midheaven (♂ ✳ △), you may have success with a career in the arts. Some possibilities include music, dance, painting, sculpting, acting, or design. A financial career is another option. The conjunction will increase your popularity, and whatever you do comes off well. With the more stressful aspects (□ ♂°), you may have a tendency to overextend yourself.

☿ MERCURY ASPECTS

Mercury-Sun

Since Mercury never travels more than 28 degrees from the Sun, the only major aspect is the conjunction (☌). This can endow you with good communication skills and an ability to accumulate and analyze information. You may be interested in writing, teaching, or sharing your ideas with others. With a close orb (0–8 degrees), you may tend to worry too much or be anxious or nervous.

Mercury-Moon

Your instinctive nature plays an important part in all decisions with the positive aspects (☌ ✶ △) between Mercury and the Moon. Your gut feelings will guide you to the right conclusion. Versatile and adaptable, you can adopt whatever position is necessary to accomplish your goal. With the stressful aspects (□ ☍), you may be restless or have difficulty saying what you feel.

Mercury-Ascendant

You convey your thoughts easily with the positive aspects from Mercury to the Ascendant (☌ ✶ △). The conjunction will give Gemini and also Virgo traits to your personality, so you may be talkative and detail-oriented. Curious and always interested in learning, you are the perpetual student. With the more stressful aspects (□ ☍), you may be misunderstood some of the time.

Mercury-Midheaven

With the positive Mercury aspects to the Midheaven (☌ ✶ △), career choices are varied and may include writer, publicist, teacher, veterinarian, or nutritionist. Many successful authors have Mercury in aspect to the Midheaven. You may be interested in working in advertising, sales, or the health care field. With the more stressful aspects (□ ☍), you can change course more than a few times and worry about your public image.

☽ MOON ASPECTS

Moon-Sun

The conjunction (☌) will intensify your self-expression and passion for life. You tend to see things solely from your own perspective. When the Sun and Moon are sextile or trine (⚹ △), you will possess equanimity and feel comfortable in your own skin. Your carefree attitude supports good health and a long life. With the stressful aspects (□ ☍), energy ebbs and flows, so learn to pace yourself.

Moon-Ascendant

Sensitive and maternal, you want to shelter and care for loved ones, animals, or anyone who needs help. The positive aspects (☌ ⚹ △) from the Moon to the Ascendant enhance your imagination. The conjunction will add personality traits of the sign of Cancer, so you may be shy and emotional. With the more stressful aspects (□ ☍), you may cling tenaciously even when it's best to let go.

Moon-Midheaven

Your career may involve the public sector or put you before the public, as in show business. With the positive Moon aspects to the Midheaven (☌ ⚹ △), you or your work can gain recognition. Possible career choices include real estate development, hotel management, and the food or restaurant business. Even the stressful aspects (□ ☍) can attract public attention, but it may be unwanted or sporadic.

☉ SUN ASPECTS

Sun-Ascendant

Your confidence and enthusiasm will attract attention when the Sun makes a positive aspect to your Ascendant (☌ ⚹ △). With the conjunction, you can exhibit Leo personality traits, so you like the limelight and revel in the recognition. You can be fearless and determined in pursuing what you want. With the more stressful aspects (□ ☍), you can appear self-centered or egotistical.

Sun-Midheaven

Your career is a personal reflection of who you are when the Sun aspects the Midheaven. A fine reputation and the respect of your peers is important to you, no matter what the occupation. Career choices are as diverse as the arts, entertainment, or business. With the positive aspects (♂ ✶ △), you can use your authority wisely and gain admiration. With stressful aspects (□ ☍), you may have to learn diplomacy.

CONCLUSION

In examining the various elements of your horoscope, keep in mind that it is a representation of the whole of you, and, as such, it may take a while to integrate all the parts to form a complete picture. Often, the bits and pieces may seem to be contradictory. This is most noticeable when two or more planets are in the same house or sign. It simply means that you have multiple energies working together, that each influences the other, and that together they symbolize the complex, multi-layered genius that is you.

With the Sun in the first house, we might say you are theatrical, lively, and happy to be the center of attention. But if Saturn is also there—especially if it is in the same sign or conjunct the Sun—then you will be a lot more reserved. Though you may still enjoy attention, this combination suggests a serious approach to attaining the recognition you want. The Sun symbolizes enthusiasm, and Saturn, self-restraint. This may seem contradictory, but it's not. Both elements are there and are expressed through your personality. So we might describe you as a person who shows great strength, persistence, and pride in your accomplishments.

It may take you some time to become familiar with your horo-scope—this is as it should be. Because just as there is no way to know someone at first glance, the process of recognizing the sum total of who you are may take a lifetime. Nothing in life is fated. You attract everything through your choices, attitudes, and patterns of thought. Most people are not consciously aware of how they create their lives, and that's why astrology is such an empowering body of knowledge. It is a visual illustration of your potential. You have chosen this time and place to enter your physical body. Make the most of it and enjoy the journey.

GLOSSARY

air signs: The air signs are ♊ Gemini, ♎ Libra, and ♒ Aquarius. The three air signs are associated with mental activity and the dissemination of information. They are sociable and enjoy exchanging ideas.

angles: Astrologers refer to the cusps of the first, fourth, seventh, and tenth houses as the angles of the horoscope.

angular houses: The first, fourth, seventh, and tenth houses are the angular houses of the astrological chart. They correspond to the cardinal signs of the same number: (1) Aries, (4) Cancer, (7) Libra, and (10) Capricorn. They are regarded as the action houses.

Aquarius: A fixed air sign, Aquarius is the eleventh sign of the zodiac. It is positive and masculine and is ruled by the planet Uranus. Its symbol is the water bearer, and its glyph is ♒, said to represent flowing water. The parts of the body ruled by Aquarius are the ankles and circulatory system. The key phrase for Aquarius is "I know."

Aries: A cardinal fire sign, Aries is the first sign of the zodiac. It is positive and masculine and is ruled by the planet Mars. Its symbol is the ram, and its glyph is ♈, said to represent the ram's horns. The part of the body ruled by Aries is the head, and those born under this sign are often prone to headaches. The key phrase for Aries is "I am."

Ascendant: Also called the rising sign, the Ascendant is the sign of the zodiac on the eastern horizon at the moment of birth. It defines your outer persona, image, and appearance.

aspect: An aspect is the angular relationship between two planets or between a planet and a point in the horoscope. The primary aspects are the conjunction, sextile, square, trine, and opposition.

benefic: A planet or aspect that has a harmonious influence is referred to as benefic or beneficial. Venus, Jupiter, and the Sun and the sextile and trine are termed benefic influences.

bowl pattern: A bowl pattern shows planets occupying one-half of the chart wheel. The keywords for this pattern are *independent* and *self-sufficient*.

bucket pattern: A bucket pattern shows planets occupying one-half of the chart wheel, with an isolated planet forming what looks like the handle of a bucket. Occasionally, the handle may be formed by two planets very close together, defined as a conjunction. The keywords for this pattern are *energetic* and *ambitious*.

bundle pattern: A bundle pattern shows planets bundled together, usually within the space of a trine, or 120°. The keywords for this pattern are *concentration* and *focus*.

cadent houses: The third, sixth, ninth, and twelfth houses are the cadent houses. They correspond to the mutable signs of the same number: (3) Gemini, (6) Virgo, (9) Sagittarius, and (12) Pisces. These are the houses where information is gathered and disseminated.

Cancer: A cardinal water sign, Cancer is the fourth sign of the zodiac. It is receptive and feminine and is ruled by the Moon. Its symbol is the crab, and its glyph is ♋, said to represent the two claws of the crab. The parts of the body ruled by Cancer are the breasts and stomach. The key phrase for Cancer is "I feel."

Capricorn: A cardinal earth sign, Capricorn is the tenth sign of the zodiac. It is receptive and feminine and is ruled by the planet Saturn.

Its symbol is the goat, and its glyph is ♑, said to represent a goat with a fish tail. Capricorn rules the skeletal system and particularly the knees. The key phrase for Capricorn is "I use."

cardinal signs: The four cardinal signs are Aries, Cancer, Libra, and Capricorn. Each one corresponds to the beginning of a new season. As the Sun moves into Aries, it marks the beginning of spring; into Cancer, the beginning of summer; into Libra, the beginning of fall; and into Capricorn, the beginning of winter. The cardinal signs prefer to initiate, and the keyword for this group is *action.*

conjunction: A conjunction is an aspect in which two planets or a planet and point in the horoscope are very close together (within 0–5°). The conjunction is a major aspect, combining the energies of those planets and/or points. It is considered a harmonious aspect if the two planets in conjunction blend their separate functions. The keyword for this aspect is *blending.*

cusp: A cusp is the dividing line separating a house from the preceding house. It also may refer to someone born on a day when the Sun is changing signs. June 21 is such a day, when the Sun is moving from the last degree of Gemini into Cancer. If your birthday falls on such a day, you are said to be born "on the cusp" and will exhibit traits of both signs.

degree rising: The degree rising is the degree (°) of the sign of the zodiac on the Ascendant at the time of birth.

Descendant: The Descendant is the seventh-house cusp and is opposite the Ascendant. It marks the beginning of one of the four angular houses. The sign on its cusp describes the nature of your relationships.

detriment: A planet is considered in detriment when it occupies the sign opposite the sign it rules. It is out of harmony or uneasy in this sign. The detriments are: Sun in Aquarius, Moon in Capricorn, Mercury in Sagittarius/Pisces, Venus in Scorpio/Aries, Mars in Libra, Jupiter in Gemini, Saturn in Cancer, Uranus in Leo, Neptune in Virgo, and Pluto in Taurus.

dignity: A planet is in dignity when it is in the sign it rules. It functions well and is considered strong. The dignities are: Sun in Leo, Moon in Cancer, Mercury in Gemini/Virgo, Venus in Taurus/Libra, Mars in Aries, Jupiter in Sagittarius, Saturn in Capricorn, Uranus in Aquarius, Neptune in Pisces, and Pluto in Scorpio.

earth signs: The earth signs are ♉ Taurus, ♍ Virgo, and ♑ Capricorn. The three earth signs are associated with the practical and material aspects of life. They rely on what can be verified and provide the foundation needed to establish something.

eclipse: There are two kinds of eclipses, solar and lunar. The full or partial obscuring of the Sun by the Moon is a solar eclipse, while the full or partial obscuring of the Moon by the Sun is a lunar eclipse. Eclipses often are associated with significant events in one's life.

elements: The signs of the zodiac fall into one of the four elements: fire, earth, air, and water. Fire corresponds with enthusiasm and optimism, earth corresponds with practicality and persistence, air corresponds with analysis and dissemination of information, and water corresponds with instinctive and emotional responses.

ephemeris: An ephemeris is an astrological almanac listing the astronomical positions of the Sun, Moon, and planets.

Equal House system: The Equal House system is one of many house systems used to calculate the horoscope. In this system, each of the twelve houses are equal in width.

exaltation: A planet is considered in exaltation when it is in the sign in which it functions best. The exaltations are: Sun in Aries, Moon in Taurus, Mercury in Aquarius, Venus in Pisces, Mars in Capricorn, Jupiter in Cancer, Saturn in Libra, and Uranus in Scorpio.

fall: A planet is considered in its fall when it is in the sign opposite its exalted position. A planet in its fall may have difficulty expressing its true nature. The planets in fall are: Sun in Libra, Moon in Scorpio, Mercury in Leo, Venus in Virgo, Mars in Cancer, Jupiter in Capricorn, Saturn in Aries, and Uranus in Taurus.

feminine signs: The feminine signs are described as negative or receptive. They include all the earth and water signs—Taurus, Cancer, Virgo, Scorpio, Capricorn, and Pisces. This categorization refers to polarity, as in positive/negative magnetic fields or yin/yang.

fire signs: The fire signs are ♈ Aries, ♌ Leo, and ♐ Sagittarius. The three fire signs are associated with action and inspiration. They often motivate and encourage others to reach for their goals.

fixed signs: The four fixed signs are Taurus, Leo, Scorpio, and Aquarius. The fixed signs are known for their staying power, without which it would be impossible to establish something. They tend to persist even in the face of changing circumstances and have to learn flexibility. The fixed signs will stay the course, and the keyword for this group is *stability.*

Gemini: A mutable air sign, Gemini is the third sign of the zodiac. It is positive and masculine and is ruled by the planet Mercury. Its symbol is the twins, and its glyph is ♊, said to represent two acting together. The parts of the body ruled by Gemini are the arms, hands, and lungs. The key phrase for Gemini is "I think."

glyphs: The symbols that represent the planets, signs, and other celestial bodies are called astrological glyphs.

grand cross: When four or more planets form what appears to be a cross in the pattern of the horoscope, it is referred to as a grand cross. This pattern contains at least four square aspects (90°) and two opposition aspects (180°). The grand cross is associated with a challenging set of circumstances in the life of the native, which can result in great accomplishment.

grand trine: When three or more planets form what appears to be a triangle in the pattern of the horoscope, it is called a grand trine. This pattern contains at least three planets in trine aspect (120°) to each other. The grand trine is associated with a fortunate set of circumstances in the life of the native, and the person appears to be lucky.

hard aspects: The square and opposition are the two major hard aspects, so called because they are associated with obstacles and challenges that require effort to overcome.

hemisphere: In astrology, hemisphere refers to the division of the horoscope wheel into upper and lower halves; it can be further divided into right-hand and left-hand halves. The upper half, also called the southern hemisphere, corresponds with daylight hours and is diurnal. The lower half, also called the northern hemisphere, corresponds with evening hours and is nocturnal.

horizon: The eastern horizon corresponds to the Ascendant in the horoscope, while the western horizon corresponds to the Descendant.

horoscope: The word horoscope literally means "hour watcher," from the Greek *hora* ("hour") and *skopos* ("watcher"). In contemporary astrology, it refers to the astrological chart.

houses: The houses form the basic framework of the astrological chart. They are the twelve pie-shaped divisions of the wheel separated by cusps. Each house has its own meaning and defines a different area of life experience.

> *first house:* personality, how others see me
> *second house:* money and possessions, personal resources
> *third house:* mental process, information sharing, siblings
> *fourth house:* home, family, nurturing parent, foundations
> *fifth house:* children, creative expression, fun and romance
> *sixth house:* daily work, personal service, health matters
> *seventh house:* marriage, partnerships, relating to others
> *eighth house:* shared resources, inheritance, intimacies
> *ninth house:* higher mind, travel, philosophy and religion, wisdom
> *tenth house:* career, reputation, public image, authority
> *eleventh house:* friends, group involvement, ideals and dreams
> *twelfth house:* seclusion, sacrifice, transcendence, mysticism

Imum Coeli (IC): The *Imum Coeli*, or IC, is directly opposite the Midheaven and also is called the fourth-house cusp. *Imum Coeli* (from Latin) literally means "the bottom of the sky."

ingress: Ingress refers to when one of the planets or luminaries enters a new sign. The Sun's ingress into one of the four cardinal signs (Aries, Cancer, Libra, and Capricorn) signals the beginning of one of the four seasons (spring, summer, fall, and winter, respectively).

intercepted: A condition that occurs when the houses of the birth chart are of unequal size sometimes results in a zodiac sign being "intercepted" within a house. An intercepted sign is contained wholly within a house. When this occurs, the meaning of the house reflects the influence of both the sign on the house cusp and the intercepted sign, and thus is more complex.

Jupiter: The largest planet in the solar system, in mythology Jupiter was a sky god associated with victory, wisdom, and justice. Its astrological meaning is good fortune and luck, expansion and growth. Jupiter remains in each sign of the zodiac for approximately one year and takes about twelve years to go once around the horoscope. Jupiter rules the sign of Sagittarius.

Leo: A fixed fire sign, Leo is the fifth sign of the zodiac. It is positive and masculine and is ruled by the Sun. Its symbol is the lion, and its glyph is ♌, said to represent the lion's mane. The part of the body ruled by Leo is the heart. The key phrase for Leo is "I will."

Libra: A cardinal air sign, Libra is the seventh sign of the zodiac. It is positive and masculine and is ruled by the planet Venus. Its symbol is the scales, and its glyph is ♎, said to represent the balancing scales. The parts of the body ruled by Libra are the kidneys and lower back. The key phrase for Libra is "I balance."

locomotive pattern: The locomotive pattern shows planets dispersed around two-thirds of the wheel, leaving an empty trine, or a space of 120°. The keywords for this pattern are *confidence* and *individuality*.

luminaries: The luminaries are the Sun and Moon. This term is derived from traditional references to the bodies that "lit up" the Earth.

Luna: Luna is another name for the Moon.

lunation: Astrologically, this term refers to the New Moon, whose cycle has a duration of twenty-nine days.

malefic: A planet or aspect that has an inharmonious influence is referred to as malefic or unfortunate. Traditionally, Mars and Saturn fell into this category. However, modern astrology illustrates that a planet is not malefic if properly integrated. The square and opposition—termed *hard aspects*—were referred to as malefic. The conjunction was sometimes considered malefic if the planets involved did not work well together.

Mars: Named after the Roman god of war, the planet Mars remains in a sign for approximately forty-seven days and takes a little less than two years to go once around the horoscope. The astrological meanings given to Mars are assertive and aggressive action, initiative and drive, breaking new ground, and showing the way. Mars rules the sign of Aries.

masculine signs: The masculine signs are described as positive. They include all the fire and air signs—Aries, Gemini, Leo, Libra, Sagittarius, and Aquarius. This categorization refers to polarity, as in positive/negative magnetic fields or yin/yang.

Medium Coeli (MC): *Medium Coeli* is another name for the Midheaven, or MC, which is the highest point in the astrological chart. It literally means "middle of the sky" (from Latin).

Mercury: Named after the Roman god who carried messages between the gods and humankind, Mercury has the following astrological meanings: communication on all levels, the assimilation and dissemination of information, local travel, and neighborhood and environment. Mercury is the planet nearest the Sun, and in the astrological chart, Mercury is never more than one sign away from the sign the Sun is in. Mercury remains in a sign for approximately seventeen days and travels completely around the horoscope every eighty-eight days. Mercury rules the signs of Gemini and Virgo.

Midheaven (MC): The Midheaven, or MC, is the most elevated point in the astrological chart. It also is referred to as the tenth-house cusp.

Moon: The Moon is Earth's satellite and completes an orbit of Earth once every 27.32 days. The Moon has a rich mythology but is associated primarily with Diana, the Roman goddess of fertility and child-birth. Hence, the astrological meaning of the Moon is related to all things feminine, including women, motherhood, home and family, and emotions and sensitivity. Because the Moon moves so quickly and changes signs approximately every two days, it is also associated with changes. The Moon rules the sign of Cancer.

mutable signs: The four mutable signs are Gemini, Virgo, Sagittarius, and Pisces. The mutable signs are known for their flexibility and adaptability. They are usually open-minded and can adjust easily to new situations. Sometimes referred to as the common signs, the mutable signs can be too malleable and have to learn to trust their instincts. The keyword for this group is *adaptability*.

Nadir: Nadir means the lowest point and is another name for the low point of the horoscope, or the fourth-house cusp.

natal astrology: Natal astrology is the branch of astrology in which an individual's birth chart is interpreted. It is based on the astrological influences present at the moment of birth.

natal chart: The natal chart is also called the birth chart or astrological chart. It is a map of the heavens at the moment of your birth. The map consists of symbols used to illustrate the stars, planetary positions, and other celestial influences.

nativity: Nativity is another name for the natal chart.

natural ruler: This term is used to refer to the natural association between each of the twelve signs and the twelve houses they rule. For instance, Aries is the natural ruler of the first house, Taurus is the natural ruler of the second house, and so on.

Neptune: Named after the Roman god of the sea, the planet Neptune remains in a sign for approximately fourteen years and takes about 165 years to go once around the horoscope. The astrological meanings given to Neptune are imagination and perception, compassion and sensitivity, and illusions and seclusion. Neptune rules the sign of Pisces.

northern hemisphere: The lower half of the horoscope is the northern hemisphere. It represents the nocturnal hours and the northern signs (Aries to Virgo).

opposition: An opposition is an aspect in which a planet is opposite (180°) another planet or point in the horoscope. It is a major aspect that is defined as challenging because it is necessary to cooperate or compromise with an opposing view. The opposition signifies conflict between internal and external factors. The keywords for this aspect are *awareness* and *flexibility.*

orb of influence: The orb of influence is the range within which an aspect is considered effective. Since few aspects are exact, this range is usually a few degrees within the defined distance. For example, though a square is defined as 90° between two points, the allowed range is between 85° and 95°, or five degrees on either side of exactitude. This range varies, because astrologers differ as to how large orbs should be.

Pisces: A mutable water sign, Pisces is the twelfth sign of the zodiac. It is feminine and receptive and is ruled by the planet Neptune. Its symbol is the fish, and its glyph is ♓, said to be two fish swimming in opposite directions and connected by their tails. The part of the body ruled by Pisces is the feet. The key phrase for Pisces is "I believe."

planets: The planets are celestial bodies orbiting the Sun from which we derive the astrological influences that affect humankind.

Pluto: Named after the Roman god of the underworld, Pluto was not discovered until 1930. However, similar mythologies existed much earlier in different world cultures. Pluto's astrological meanings include death and rebirth, transformation, sexuality, and hidden matters. Pluto is the planet farthest from the Sun. Because of its irregular orbit, Pluto can remain in one sign anywhere from twelve to twenty-two years and takes about 240 years to go completely around the horoscope. Pluto rules the sign of Scorpio.

quadrant: The four quadrants divide the astrological wheel into four sets of three houses. The first quadrant consists of houses 1, 2, and

3; the second quadrant consists of houses 4, 5, and 6; the third quadrant consists of houses 7, 8, and 9; and the fourth quadrant consists of houses 10, 11, and 12. Each quadrant is associated with a different area of development.

qualities: One way in which the signs of the zodiac are classified is by quality, also known as quadruplicity. The three qualities are cardinal, fixed, and mutable. The cardinal signs are Aries, Cancer, Libra, and Capricorn; the fixed signs are Taurus, Leo, Scorpio, and Aquarius; and the mutable signs are Gemini, Virgo, Sagittarius, and Pisces.

radix: Radix is another term used to describe the natal chart. It means "original" or "root" and is used to differentiate the birth chart from other types of secondary charts, such as the progressed chart.

retrograde: Retrograde refers to the apparent backward motion of a planet in its orbit. This illusion is caused by the different speeds of the orbiting planets from our perspective on Earth. To illustrate this phenomenon, see yourself sitting on a moving train while another train passes at a higher speed but going in the same direction. The illusion is that you are going backward. In a natal chart, a retrograde planet is shown with a small *R* next to its symbol. The planet's meaning remains the same, though its expression is more on the intuitive or subconscious level.

rulership: This term refers to the relationship between the planet and the sign it rules. The modern rulers are as follows: Mars rules Aries, Venus rules Taurus, Mercury rules Gemini, Moon rules Cancer, Sun rules Leo, Mercury rules Virgo, Venus rules Libra, Pluto rules Scorpio, Jupiter rules Sagittarius, Saturn rules Capricorn, Uranus rules Aquarius, and Neptune rules Pisces. Further, each house is ruled by the planet that rules the sign on its cusp.

Sagittarius: A mutable fire sign, Sagittarius is the ninth sign of the zodiac. It is masculine and positive and is ruled by the planet Jupiter. Its symbol, the centaur, is half human and half animal. Its glyph ♐ represents the arrow of spirit aimed toward the heavens in search of wisdom. Sagittarius rules the hips, thighs, and liver. The key phrase for Sagittarius is "I see."

Saturn: Named after the Roman god of agriculture, Saturn was the slowest-moving planet known to the ancients; thus, it came to symbolize time, age, and wisdom. Saturn's astrological meanings include career and occupation, planning and long-term goals, practical and material achievements, and wisdom gained through experience. Saturn remains in a sign for approximately two and a half years and takes twenty-nine years to go completely around the horoscope. Saturn rules the sign of Capricorn.

Scorpio: A fixed water sign, Scorpio is the eighth sign of the zodiac. It is feminine and receptive and is ruled by the planet Pluto. Its primary symbol is the scorpion, though it also is symbolized by the snake and the eagle. Scorpio is the only sign with multiple symbols. Its glyph is ♏, said to represent a scorpion. Scorpio rules the reproductive organs. The key phrase for Scorpio is "I desire."

seesaw pattern: Like the name implies, the seesaw pattern shows two opposing groups of planets with a space of at least 90° on either side of the grouping. The keywords for this pattern are *awareness* and *compromise.*

sextile: A sextile is an aspect in which two planets or a planet and point in the horoscope are 60° apart. A sextile is a major aspect that is defined as harmonious. The energies of both planets may work well together, though their qualities may have to be developed further. The keyword for this aspect is *opportunity.*

singleton: The isolated planet that forms the handle of a bucket pattern is called the singleton.

soft aspects: The sextile and trine are the two major soft aspects, so called because they are associated with benefit and opportunity.

solar chart: A solar chart is based on the location of the Sun on the day of birth. In the absence of a birth time, astrologers place the Sun's degree on the Ascendant and then calculate the succeeding houses in equal arcs of 30°. The solar chart is interpreted in the same way as a natal chart would be.

southern hemisphere: The upper half of the horoscope is the southern hemisphere. It represents the diurnal hours and the southern signs (Libra to Pisces).

splash pattern: A splash pattern is one in which the planets are dispersed around the wheel with most of the signs occupied. The splash pattern shows someone who has widespread interests, and the keywords for this pattern are *versatility* and *universality*.

splay pattern: The splay pattern is one in which the planets are distributed in an irregular fashion. It has elements of many of the other chart patterns but does not quite fit into any one of them. It may have three areas of emphasis, and the keywords for this pattern are *self-reliant* and *artistic*.

square: A square is an aspect in which a planet is 90° from another planet or point in the horoscope. A square is a major aspect that is defined as challenging because it represents internal conflict symbolized by the planets involved in the aspect. The keywords for the square are *internal conflict* and *tension*.

star: A star is a self-luminous celestial body, such as our Sun, as differentiated from the planets, which reflect light.

stellium: A stellium is three or more planets in conjunction with one another (within 0–5°). The planets are usually in the same sign and house. This combination places emphasis on the matters of the house in which it occurs and the sign it is in.

succedent houses: The second, fifth, eighth, and eleventh houses are the succedent houses. They succeed the angular houses and correspond to the fixed signs of the same number: (2) Taurus, (5) Leo, (8) Scorpio, and (11) Aquarius. They are the houses where resources are developed.

Sun: Sol from Roman mythology was the Sun god who drove his chariot across the sky every day and thus was associated with constancy and loyalty. The Sun is the center of our solar system and the most prominent celestial body. The Sun's astrological meanings include self-expression and self-image, life-force, and individuality. The Sun remains in a sign for one day and takes 365 days, or one year, to go completely around the horoscope. The Sun rules the sign of Leo.

Sun sign: The sign of the zodiac the Sun is in on the date of birth is called the Sun sign or birth sign. Since the Sun is considered the most important influence in one's horoscope, the sign that the Sun occupies is of utmost importance in the birth chart.

T-square: When three or more planets form what appears to be a *T* in the pattern of the horoscope, it is referred to as a T-square. This pattern contains two planets in opposition (180°) to one another and a third planet—usually halfway between the other two—forming a square (90°) to each of them. The T-square is associated with a challenging set of circumstances in the life of the native. The house at the open end of the T formation is usually an area of life in which much can be achieved.

Taurus: A fixed earth sign, Taurus is the second sign of the zodiac. It is feminine and receptive and is ruled by the planet Venus. Its symbol is the bull, and its glyph is ♉, said to represent a bull's head and horns. Taurus rules the throat and vocal cords. The key phrase for Taurus is "I have."

trine: A trine is an aspect in which a planet is 120° from another planet or point in the horoscope. A trine is a major aspect that is defined as harmonious and beneficial. It represents ease and accord between the planets involved and is associated with good fortune. The keywords for this aspect are *harmony* and *luck.*

triplicity: This term refers to three signs of the same element: the fire triplicity (Aries, Leo, and Sagittarius), the earth triplicity (Taurus, Virgo, and Capricorn), the water triplicity (Cancer, Scorpio, and Pisces), and the air triplicity (Gemini, Libra, and Aquarius).

Uranus: Named after the Greek god of the sky, Uranus was the first planet to be discovered beyond Saturn and thus changed traditional wisdom regarding astronomy and astrology. Uranus came to be associated with unorthodox and unconventional thinking. It is the planet that rules astrology, among other things. Uranus remains in a sign for approximately seven years and takes eighty-four years to go completely around the horoscope. Uranus rules the sign of Aquarius.

Venus: Named after the Roman goddess of love, beauty, and fertility, Venus orbits between the Earth and Sun and never appears to be far from the Sun. Venus therefore is never more than two signs away from your Sun sign. Venus mythology also is associated with sensuality, possessions, and money. This planet remains in a sign for approximately twenty-four days and takes about 244 days to go completely around the horoscope.

Virgo: A mutable earth sign, Virgo is the sixth sign of the zodiac. It is feminine and receptive and is ruled by the planet Mercury. Its symbol is the virgin, and its glyph is ♍, said to represent a young woman with crossed legs. Virgo rules the nervous system. The key phrase for Virgo is "I analyze."

water signs: The water signs are ♋ Cancer, ♏ Scorpio, and ♓ Pisces. The three water signs are associated with intuition, sensitivity, and emotion. They embody the traits of compassion and nurturing.

zenith: The zenith is the celestial point directly overhead from any location on Earth. It often is confused with the Midheaven, which is the most elevated point in the astrological chart.

zodiac: The zodiac is a circular band or belt that comprises the twelve signs: Aries, Taurus, Gemini, Cancer, Leo, Virgo, Libra, Scorpio, Sagittarius, Capricorn, Aquarius, and Pisces. The zodiac extends around the Earth on the line of the ecliptic (the path of Earth's orbit).

TO WRITE TO THE AUTHOR

If you wish to contact the author or would like more information about this book, please write to the author in care of Llewellyn Worldwide and we will forward your request. Both the author and publisher appreciate hearing from you and learning of your enjoyment of this book and how it has helped you. Llewellyn Worldwide cannot guarantee that every letter written to the author can be answered, but all will be forwarded. Please write to:

Joann Hampar
℅ Llewellyn Worldwide
2143 Wooddale Drive, Dept. 978-0-7387-1106-5
Woodbury, Minnesota 55125-2989, U.S.A.

Please enclose a self-addressed stamped envelope for reply,
or $1.00 to cover costs. If outside U.S.A., enclose
international postal reply coupon.

Many of Llewellyn's authors have websites with additional information and resources. For more information, please visit our website at http://www.llewellyn.com.

FREE BIRTH CHART OFFER
FROM LLEWELLYN

Thank you for purchasing one of Llewellyn's popular astrology titles. Astrology is an extremely valuable tool for gaining a deeper understanding of your gifts, talents, challenges, and tasks for this lifetime. Llewellyn's Professional Natal Chart—a *visual* representation of your birth chart—is the perfect starting point for your journey of self-discovery.

As an added bonus, by ordering your free chart you'll be enrolled in Llewellyn's Birthday Club! Just write "Birthday Club" on your order form. Membership in the Birthday Club entitles you to 25% off any of Llewellyn's astrology reports when you order within one month of your birthday.

Complete this form with your birth data and mail it to the address below. It's very important to have accurate information, so you may want to refer to your birth certificate to get your exact birth time. Enjoy your adventure in self-discovery through astrology!

Please do not photocopy this form. Only the original will be accepted. Thank you.

PLEASE PRINT

Full Name:_____

Mailing Address: _____

              City,   State,   Zip

Birth Time: _____ A.M. or P.M. (please circle one)

Month:_____ Day:_____ Year:_____

Birthplace (City, County, State, Country): _____

_____

Mail to:

Llewellyn Worldwide, Special Chart Offer

2143 Wooddale Drive

Woodbury, MN 55125-2989

Please allow 4–6 weeks for delivery